Danvers State

Memoirs Of A Nurse In The Asylum

By

Angelina Szot and Barbara Stilwell

Editing: Eileen Roche

authorHOUSE™

1663 LIBERTY DRIVE, SUITE 200
BLOOMINGTON, INDIANA 47403
(800) 839-8640
WWW.AUTHORHOUSE.COM

First published by AuthorHouse 11/16/04

ISBN: 1-4184-9136-5 (e)
ISBN: 1-4184-9135-7 (sc)
ISBN: 1-4184-9134-9 (dj)

Library of Congress Control Number: 2004096219

Printed in the United States of America
Bloomington, Indiana

This book is printed on acid-free paper.

TABLE OF CONTENTS

CHAPTER 1

Choosing a Less Chosen Path

It was in 1948 that I applied for a job at Danvers State Hospital, an asylum in Massachusetts. Even back then its time worn buildings held a long history. Danvers had been a state institution for the insane for many, many years. It had acquired an aura of mystique that had become a source of local fascination. The facility was completely isolated from the surrounding communities, sitting high on a hill surrounded by a large tract of wooded land. The trees obscured its physical presence. It lay hidden like some long ignored malignancy. The main drive leading up to Danvers was a winding, narrow road gradually ascending to the main gates. The entrance brought to mind visions of the entrance to Dante's inferno. My first impression of the facility was one of awe. Despite the feelings of trepidation I had, the almost inappropriate grandeur and elegance of the buildings overwhelmed me. At the top, Danvers stood like some gothic castle, a forbidding structure that served as a solid reminder of how much people had always feared and shunned madness. Thick stone walls guarded the melancholy secrets of that place. Despite its seclusion, everyone in the area knew of the insane asylum high up on the hill. It was a place shrouded in modern day myth and legend, a place that in time would leave its indelible mark on me.

Danvers was built in 1874, with additions added on over the decades. By the 1940's it had been rapidly aged by the rough New England weather; it appeared somehow ancient. Masses of creeping vines wound their way up the stone walls that had taken on a dull gray tint. The sprawling complex that comprised the institution included a cemetery and a farm nestled besides its forty buildings. It was its own closed community. It was huge, and such an anomaly, with its weathered but pristine appearance hiding the squalor and human sadness that lay inside. When I looked at it for the first time, I felt the visceral fear I believe all of us have when confronting something so far removed from what we consider normal.

I made the decision to seek work at Danvers because my husband and I needed the money, and there were no other jobs available. It was desperation that had set me on a path that would take me over two decades to travel. After World War II had ended, all the soldiers and sailors had come home and filled up the jobs. Even menial jobs at factories were hard to come by. Most of the women who had taken jobs during the war quit to become housewives once the men got back, but I didn't have that luxury. My husband and I were the working poor; I had no choice but to work. We had no college degrees, no thought about careers. I had been a young bride, just nineteen. My husband, Steve, was from immigrant parents like me. I had left school in the eighth grade to stay home with my mother while she was ill and had never gone back. That had been the extent of my formal education. My husband had graduated from high school. It wasn't until years later that he took some college courses, but he never got a degree. So the two of us needed to work at whatever jobs we could get with our limited education and training.

I didn't lack ambition or a willingness to do hard work; but it was a truly different world back then. My parents had come from Italy. They both grew up in the same area just outside of Naples. Like so many of their neighbors, they had little hope and little to dream for at home, so they immigrated to the United States when they were young adults. They had to leave behind so much, but to them it seemed a fair price for the chance to be Americans. My grandchildren can't comprehend how anyone could leave their home and family to take such a long and sometimes dangerous voyage for an uncertain life. Being third generation Americans, they don't appreciate what a great and wonderful home their great-grandparents found for them. The myriad opportunities available to them didn't exist for my parents, or even for me. My world was one of structure and limitations.

I believe that many other factors also affected my decision to choose Danvers. Only in hindsight can I now see how events in my younger days strengthened those qualities inside me that would make a career at Danvers possible. My life would be far from the norm compared to the other women I knew. I found it easy to stray from the status quo, and I had a determination to prove myself by taking on the challenges I would come up against. This resolve formed early as I grew up. Restrictions were considered a necessity for girls growing up in our immigrant neighborhood.

My mother ran the household and raised the children, but it was my father who dominated our family life. Father was a tightfisted man who guarded every penny fiercely. Once a week the family would go to downtown Lawrence, an old mill town in the Merrimack Valley region of Massachusetts, to shop for the week. We'd take the bus from the nearby town of Methuen. Father would look for sales at the outdoor market. Sometimes we'd stop at this one house where a woman sold day old bread and cookies. Often the cookies would be broken up and a bit on the stale side, but they were a grand luxury for my brothers and me. Green peppers were usually a cheap item, so they were a staple in our home, used for sandwiches for work and school. On Monday we'd have eggs and peppers; on Tuesday, sausage and peppers; on Wednesday, fried peppers and onions. My father could be downright innovative with that vegetable. Years later I would see this same culinary inventiveness at Danvers where the kitchen staff endeavored to make appetizing meals with the bulk supplies given by the state.

My brothers and I were grateful to have full stomachs, but when I got married I told my husband that I planned to have variety in our meals. That would be just one of many things that I planned to change when I started my own home. Each evening meal had been planned in my father's house. Saturday was for hot dogs and beans, Sunday would be macaroni, Monday would be green soup, Tuesday would be macaroni, Wednesday was fish, Thursday macaroni again. Friday was always leftovers day. We never deviated from the meal plan. But father always made sure he bought his grapes. He used to make his own wine. He'd also buy alcohol and made spirits for the holidays. My father and brothers often went fishing on the Merrimac River. They would bring home fish and oftentimes eels. We'd bottle the eels for the winter, along with peppers and fruits. I still remember watching the pieces of eel hopping around in the frying pan as if they were still alive. All this was normal in our neighborhood. This was the way everyone lived.

There had never been any plans for me to get a college education or have a career. My father saw no need for a woman to be well educated. He also saw no need to spend money on learning. He hated spending money on just about anything. My father's parsimony wasn't limited to food. Whenever my mother bought a new dress for me, she would hide it away for a couple of weeks. Then, if my father made a comment when I finally wore the dress, my mother would say that it was a dress I had for some time. This way, she wouldn't be lying to my father; but she wouldn't have to argue with him about spending money. My husband's family had to be frugal as well, and so didn't encourage spending for a college education. Steady employment, even at a place as spooky as Danvers State, was a wonderful thing. And certainly better than working at one of the many mills that filled the Merrimack Valley back then. I was well aware of what work at the mills was like. I started working at one when I was just sixteen. Hours of mind numbing work under the steady drone of the gargantuan machines sucked the life out of me. Compared to the mills, an insane asylum that created local lore about the darkest places people can go seemed like a real opportunity.

All this happened so long ago, but the memories are still vivid. Sometimes I'll see something on the television or hear a story that touches those old remembrances. Even certain smells can bring on a feeling of nostalgia. In the winter, my mother used to place orange peels on the stove in the kitchen. We used that stove for both cooking and heating. The scent of the melting peels would drift throughout our small home. Today I throw orange peels into the fireplace of the home I share with my youngest daughter and her family. As the peels curl up and melt into the fire, the aroma takes me back more than a half century. This is when I like to share my stories with my daughter and grandchildren. The grandchildren especially like hearing tales of grandma and the "crazy" people of Danvers State Hospital.

CHAPTER 2

Taking Up the Challenge

Taking a job at Danvers State wasn't something I had ever considered in my younger days. Growing up, I never imagined a career in nursing, much less dealing with the insane. In fact, I never imagined much beyond getting married and having children one day. It had been my mother's illness that had formed my life long interest in caring for people. At the time I didn't see what a strong impact the final years of her life would have on my future life's work.

I had been the only girl in my family. My parents married shortly after they came to this country at the turn of the century. Their wedding portrait hangs in my living room. Photos were rare then, so it's the only picture I have of them. Neither spoke English when they arrived, though they eventually learned. Italian was always spoken at home. Both became citizens. They brought with them all the old ways of thinking, and not much else. My mother had always been a sickly woman for as long as I could remember. So the burden of caring for home and family gradually fell more and more to me as I grew older and my mother grew sicker. I didn't mind because I loved helping my mother, and I enjoyed the time we spent together. In the evenings I would brush my mother's long hair and put it into braids. I remember the silken feel of her hair as we talked about our hopes and desires. I never dreamed about nursing, mostly about finding the perfect man to love me and raise a large family. My father thought that it was a waste for a girl to go to school, but my mother insisted that I get as much education as possible. I got my desire to improve myself and learn all that I could straight from her. She was the one who instilled in me a yearning to seek out life's possibilities and to never erect fences around myself by thinking anything was beyond my grasp. She tried to give me all the chances she could despite her failing health and her own restricted life. She used to say to me, "As long as I'm alive, you'll never go to work. I'll try to make life easier for you." That all ended when my mother died the year I turned sixteen. As soon as her funeral was over, my father sent me to work at a local mill. I don't believe he did this with malice. I believe he thought he was choosing the right path for me – I'd already dropped out of school, so what I needed was employment. A steady paycheck would certainly help the family. He must have thought that the discipline and experience I would get from a job would mean more in my life than going back to school.

Even at the young age of sixteen I had already seen many of the harsh realities of the world. I saw how brutal life had been on my mother. Bearing fifteen children for my father had taken its toll on her. Not all of my mother's children survived. Six died either during pregnancy or at birth. Two others died in early childhood from scarlet fever. We were fortunate. Some families lost many more than two children to diseases that aren't even heard of today. Mother would breast feed the babies, which prevented her from getting pregnant. As soon as she finished breastfeeding, she'd get pregnant again. All the children were two years apart. We were pretty typical for an immigrant family. Illness and death were always close by.

I was still working at the wood mill when Steve and I got married. I hated the job that my father had forced on me, so when Steve suggested I look elsewhere, that's what I did. Of course, with my limited education and experience, I didn't have too many choices. I got a job at a shoe factory, but I hated it just as much as the mill job, so Steve told me to look elsewhere, again. The next job I got was at a tire factory. Back then, the work was grueling. We worked on assembly lines that never stopped. If you've ever seen that old "I Love Lucy" episode where she falls behind on the chocolate assembly line, you know what my working conditions were like. We were never allowed to walk away from our positions, even to go to the bathroom. When the need got urgent, we would have to ask a supervisor to find us a temporary replacement. The pay was abysmal, and the hours were long. Finally, I told Steve I couldn't stand it anymore. I quit the factory that very day, knowing I would need to find work again soon. After that I stayed home while Steve worked. Unfortunately, he got laid off. That's when he got a job at Danvers State Hospital as a male attendant. There was no such thing as a male nurse in the late 1940's.

Steve would come home from work and share his stories about the foul conditions and bizarre behavior he faced each day. I remember hearing the nervousness in Steve's voice when he would tell about having to help out when a patient got beyond the control of the attending nurse. My husband was six feet tall and weighed close to two hundred pounds. I knew it took a lot to make him feel fear. Still, I secretly thought that he might have spiced up his stories a bit to make them more interesting. So when Steve mentioned that Danvers had job openings, I thought it would be great to work and commute together. "Angie, you can do what you want, but Danvers is going to be a real eye opener for you." That was certainly throwing down the gauntlet! So I told Steve, "I'm going down there, and I'm getting a job." This was a challenge I couldn't refuse. I hated being told that I couldn't do something, especially when my husband Steve was doing the telling. He was the one who had instilled in me a strong sense of self-confidence and self-reliance in the first place.

Steve gave me all the confidence in the world. He taught me how to drive, which was a very big deal at the time, since most of the women I knew did not have a license. They all depended on their husbands or took buses. I needed the independence since I would need to work. Steve taught me how to be self-sufficient. He also let me keep my own paycheck (a very big deal back in the forties). You see, I grew up in the Merrimack Valley in Massachusetts in a very traditional immigrant family in a very traditional town. During the 1930's and 1940's, Lawrence was a large city with stores and restaurants crowded on Essex Street. The communities surrounding it were just small towns. The Valley was full of European immigrants. There were several Italian Bakeries on Common Street, French cathedrals, and Polish social clubs. We attended a church which held Italian mass. Everybody followed unspoken rules, and fathers were the final authority on everything. My husband's attitude and opinions were a dramatic change from what I had been raised with. Steve didn't want a quiet housekeeper and cook, he wanted an equal partner for the journey.

I thought that applying to Danvers would be like applying for a job at one of the factories, but I was dead wrong. At the factories a person just had to fill out a simple application. There would be much more involved in my getting a job at Danvers. I didn't have much time to think about that, though. We stretched Steve's paycheck as far as it would go, but we were always a little bit short, and there was no chance to save any money. My dreams of a house and large family would have to wait until I started working again.

We were always on the brink of disaster. Our finances were so tight. When we needed to fix up the old jalopy we had for a car, Steve would go to the junkyard and rummage through the heaps of discarded cars and parts, doing most of the repairs himself. Yet we still managed to keep a clean, comfortable home and eat well. And once I started working again we were able to support the children I had always wanted. Even though we had to stretch every penny to the limit, it was worth it to hear their giggles and see them sleeping peacefully at night. Especially because I thought I would never have those kinds of wonderful moments.

We had breezed along happily married, but longing for children. I never used any form of birth control, but I was unable to get pregnant. Since I had no mother to confide in, I patiently waited for the good Lord to help me along. Finally, after three years, I conceived. Yet almost immediately, I miscarried. This happened three times. Steve had me go to a doctor to find out what was wrong. I was told that I would never be able to have children. I accepted the fact and went on with my life.

Shortly after that I found myself pregnant again. This time I carried full term and gave birth to my oldest, Teresa (named after my mother). Six months later I started feeling ill. I went to see the doctor to find out what was wrong. As soon as he saw me, he said, "You're pregnant!" I thought he was crazy, but nine months later my second daughter, Linda, was born. Now I had two children who were just fifteen months apart. Not bad for a woman who couldn't have children.

Now money was even tighter than it had been in the earlier days. So that's why Steve suggested that I try to get a job at Danvers State, if all else failed. We both knew I would never be a stay at home mother. So I went "up the hill", convinced I'd get hired.

CHAPTER 3

Going Up The Hill

I was actually excited about applying to Danvers State. Besides the fact that I had something I wanted to prove to my husband, I thought that I would enjoy working closely with people who needed me. Caring for the sick seemed to come naturally to me. I didn't get easily squeamish, and I got a real satisfaction out of comforting those who were suffering. I probably first realized this when my mother was still alive, since she turned out to be my first patient. I may have had some Florence Nightingale fantasy about how wonderful the job would be. I never realized what would be involved in caring for people who were often a lot sicker than my mother had ever been. I had believed that dealing with my mother's illness and death had prepared me for whatever I might face. I would eventually come to know just how deep pain and suffering could be. I would see the agonies the human body can endure as well as the tortures that afflict the mind. Fortunately, I had no clue whatsoever about those things, so I giddily set off to get myself the job.

Resumes weren't required to apply, which was a real plus since I had no idea how to make one. There was a general application to complete. Experience wasn't required either. Danvers State provided on the job training for aides. I thought this would be the easiest thing in the world. I was one hundred percent positive that I would be working there by the following Monday. I ended up working harder to get that job than for anything else I had ever tried before.

I drove up the hill by myself. Steve's tales about his work there, at times harrowing, at times comical, had me steeled for my first entrance. The front office where all visitors went was a clean and cheerful place, which struck me as rather odd. I suppose I had imagined some kind of dungeon with dim lights and an aura of baleful hopelessness. Stories of crazed murderers and people who lived in imaginary worlds speaking to others no one else could see were part of the area's history. Even I wasn't immune to the mystery of this local curiosity. I asked the woman in the front office for an application. I was so excited thinking about how good life would be once the paychecks started coming in. Thirty-eight dollars per week was damn good money at the time. Plus there were overlapping shifts which provided twenty four hour coverage on the wards, so there were different shift options that might allow me and Steve to work out a schedule for commuting and taking care of the children. This was going to be so good.

I filled out my application and turned it in. That's when I was told that all the openings had been filled; my application would be kept on file. I couldn't believe it. It was as if my heart stopped beating for a few seconds. This was something that had never dawned on me as being possible. But there was no way I was going to give up all those beautiful fantasies I had played out in my mind already. Determination set in me like concrete. As I made the drive home alone, I thought about what I could possibly do to fix the situation. I came up with an idea that seemed perfectly reasonable to me.

I was so desperate, I contacted my local Congressman. I was a taxpaying voter in dire straits. I explained my situation and pleaded for some help. I wasn't even speaking with the Congressman, just some office aide. But I didn't care. Getting this job was a necessity.

For some bizarre and wonderful reason, the Congressman decided to help me. His office checked out the situation, and, miraculously, I was called back in to the front office at Danvers. To this day I don't know how or why I was helped. I was offered a job, and I thought this was a special turning point in my life.

CHAPTER 4

The First Day

I couldn't believe how enthused I was about going to Danvers for my first day at work. This was going to be so different from working at the factories or mills. I was actually going to be learning skills instead of spending long hours doing mind numbing, repetitive tasks. This would also be the first time that I would actually be inside the facility beyond the comfortable front offices. I had an overwhelming curiosity about the place, especially after hearing Steve's stories. I started on the day shift while I was being trained, so I would see everything in bright daylight. I could hardly believe how lucky I was and how much I had to look forward to. Even with all the struggles over money, I still had so much that was wonderful in my life. Yet, all the joy I felt was tempered with some sad memories of my mother. I couldn't help but reflect on what she had lived through now that I was going down a road she never had a chance to choose.

My life was a far cry from the one my mother had lived. She and her three sisters came to the U.S. through Ellis Island. They were herded off the ship and into the main building. Like all immigrants, my mother and her sisters were "inspected" as soon as they got off the boat. They were checked for any obvious physical or mental shortcomings. One of my aunts, Consiglia, was not allowed to enter the country because she was mentally "slow". She had to return to Italy. It was as simple as that. Only the sturdiest and most capable workers were allowed to stay. It was a heart wrenching time for the sisters, though they all remained in touch through the years. My mother's parents had remained in Italy, so her unlucky sister would not be alone. So my mother began her new life in America without money, parents, an education, or a job. I felt blessed to be in my precarious situation!

My first day "on the wards" was a true revelation to me. I soon found that Steve had understated the conditions I would find. The wards were scary – dark and gloomy, full of people unfit for the outside world. It seemed as if the daylight couldn't penetrate this hidden enclave that appeared to be bursting with people. There were one hundred and fifty patients crammed on each floor. Even to a novice like me it was obvious that the wards were designed for far fewer patients. It reminded me of one of the early apartments my parents had rented. My six brothers shared a single bedroom. Since

I was the only girl, I got my own room. It was heaven for me even though that bedroom was barely larger than a modern bathroom. There was just enough room for one bureau and a single bed. Still, it was stately luxury compared to the cramped beds of my brothers. They slept three to a bed, with both beds in a single room. Danvers was appallingly familiar. There was a strange melancholy about the swarms of patients I saw. It definitely wasn't the teeming, lively crowd I'd seen at the downtown stores or bustling about at the open produce markets.

The place was also filled with unfamiliar odors. The stench of unwashed bodies mingled with the smells of food and medications. I realized immediately that there were patients who couldn't control their bodies, with the foul miasma of urine and feces mingled in with the rest of the onslaught in the air. I tried breathing through my mouth, doubting I would ever get used to the smell. In time I would come to recognize every scent of the place, from the antiseptic cleaning fluids to the foulness of gangrene.

There was also the unending cacophony of the daily routines. Aids pushing carts, patients having conversations with no one in particular, the nurses giving orders. The barrage of noises was disconcerting. Was there any order at all to this place? I learned that despite the appearance of chaos, there was actually a very well defined order to the typical day.

Since I was new to Danvers, I didn't fully participate in the daily rituals. I was given a brief tour and introduced to the staff. The aides were all friendly, but the nurses were very formal. Their stiff introductions gave me quick notice about the pecking order I would work under. I did learn that during the day, shortly after breakfast, the patients would all be brought out onto the porch, a big long sun porch. Except, of course, those few patients too ill or too dangerous to be brought out. It would be some time before I would be introduced to the patients who couldn't associate with the untrained aides or the more sedate patients. I couldn't understand at the time why there were aides constantly hovering around watching the people on the porch. The patients all appeared calm and well behaved. Why were they being treated like convicts in a high security prison?

A tour of the facility made me realize that the sun porch and back wards weren't that bad. Bad was one of the violent wards. The majority of aides there were men. Big, burly men with quick reflexes. On these wards I saw people throwing their own crap. I was utterly shocked by seeing this strange behavior. One aide told me, "Most of the time we can see it flying, and we just have to duck." These women made it sound as if avoiding flying feces were the most normal thing in the world!

I was told that the patients would often attack each other or the staff in the violent sections. It was hard for me to imagine such a thing. I was grateful I was going to avoid working those wards, having been assigned to another area. Just the quick glimpse of those areas was enough to set my mind against working in them. In time I would come to know the people on those wards. I'd learn their sorrowful tales and see their humanity.

I learned that the day shift needed to take patients to the showers. This was a big, big room, not individual stalls. I had never seen anything like it. Large showerheads jutted from the bare walls; filthy water made its way down the large drain holes. It took three aides to clean the patients. The whole process fascinated me. The aides had to put on bathing suits. Two aides would go into the shower and wash the patients one at a time, scrubbing their bodies from head to toe with soap, then wash their hair. The third aide would stand outside on watch, prepared to sound the alarm if things ever got out of control, or if there were a medical emergency. I was informed that this happened at least once a week, someone sounding the alarm. I tried to picture what it would be like to deal with a situation while barefoot and dressed in a bathing suit, dripping and exposed. Definitely needed to keep my mind from wandering.

My tour continued with a visit to the cafeteria and some of the other areas. The facility was enormous. I could barely take in everything I saw and heard. I found myself mesmerized watching the doctors and nurses. But I did end my day with a sense of something almost like foreboding. Danvers was just so immense and so strange. And so scary. Would I really be able to handle the job? I kept my concerns to myself. No point in telling Steve about my worries since I had so boldly bragged about being able to handle anything that Danvers might dish out. Though I did give a little more credence to the stories he had told me about his "adventures" at work. I only hoped my days would be less eventful.

CHAPTER 5

The Novice Aide

As I continued my first week at Danvers I found that the veteran aides were very willing to describe the routine of the asylum, for which I was deeply thankful. I learned that there was plenty of information one needed that wasn't provided at orientation or training. It seemed everyone had some tidbit of knowledge that made the work easier, or safer.

I was still thinking about what kind of work schedule would work best for Steve and me. I had a husband and children to consider in the equation. After my initial training I would have the option of picking another shift, although the senior aides got first dibs. I learned that each shift had its own pros and cons. It went down to two girls and a nurse for the graveyard shift. That was the shift between the normal morning shift and the late night shift. There wouldn't be much help if an emergency came up, but the other aides said that it was normally quiet and pretty easy work if you could get used to the hours. The graveyard shift crew mostly monitored the wards and prepared paperwork. The two day shifts required plenty of stamina, because that was when most of the patient care was needed, such as feeding and bathing. And other duties I wasn't told about that first day. It wasn't long before I got my first introduction to one of these additional tasks.

After only three days on the job, another girl asked for my help with a patient. I casually said, "Yeah, I'll help you." I thought she needed help lifting someone up or changing soiled clothes. In just a short space of time I came to the conclusion that most of the patients were incontinent! I went into the room and said, "Gee, what are you doing to her?"

"I got to clean her up."

The woman was lying naked on the bed, completely still. The other aide began wiping her down, lifting her limp arms and scrubbing the flesh with harsh, brisk wipes. She wanted my help turning the patient over. I thought the poor woman should at least be covered up, giving her some small piece of dignity while we performed this necessary violation. This seemed such a humiliating way to treat an old woman, even if she couldn't perform the simplest hygiene and didn't understand what was going on.

The other aide said, "Don't worry about it, Szot."

When I turned the patient over the air came out of her chest with a sighing sound.

I said, "She looks like she's dead."

The other aide said, "That's because she is dead, Szot."

This was at 6 o'clock in the morning; I could have died myself. At that time I had never seen anyone die except my mother and father, and I had never handled a dead body before. I had assumed the woman had been in some kind of stupor. Working so intimately with the dead gave me an eerie feeling. It also brought back the most terrible memories of when my own mother had passed.

My mother had always been a physically frail woman. She had been diagnosed with a heart condition that left her bedridden. She had been taking medication for her weak heart. When father brought her to a specialist, it was discovered that she had a tumor the size of a baby. And she did not have a heart problem. We learned that her heart medication had actually weakened her heart. The new doctor said he would need to drain the fluid built up inside my mother, then he could operate to remove the tumor. He would start

29

treatment the next day. That very night my mother passed away. I was just sixteen. That had been my first experience with death. It was a remote one, with other people handling the preparation of the body and the funeral arrangements. I saw my mother's lifeless body up close at the wake, and that had affected me deeply. As was tradition, I touched her arm briefly as I knelt before her casket to offer a prayer. Now I was expected to do all kinds of things with a dead body. Granted, since this patient was a complete stranger to me it was a bit easier for me to handle the idea. But I still had a cold knot of dread inside me.

I knew nothing about preparing the dead, what we referred to then as cadavers for the morgue. The other aide needed to explain the process. At that time we first had to wash patients from top to bottom, hair and everything. They had to be clean for the undertaker. When the other aide told me this I felt a chill run through me. I had never been this close to death. Touching the cold flesh and stiffening limbs spurred me to work quickly. I wasn't even sure if I could finish. The other aide just kept chit chatting merrily along while I desperately tried to keep my eyes from looking into the dead woman's lifeless stare. Was I really scrubbing the scalp and private parts of this lifeless body? Nothing could have been worse, except possibly the next step in the process.

Once the body had been thoroughly washed, we had to stuff all openings - nostrils, ears, vagina, and rectum - with cotton. If there were any fluids left in the body, the stuffing would prevent it from coming out. The other aide explained that it would be worse to have to clean up dried snot or spots of crap later. Picturing this image in my mind certainly removed any qualms I had had about ramming wads of cotton into this poor woman. Of course, being able to do it didn't stop my stomach from turning over. I thought for sure my queasiness was going to end up in an explosion of vomit at any second. And still the other aide kept talking away, oblivious to the fact that she was working on a corpse.

Finally the hardest part was over. Next was the step of positioning the body in a specific way according to the patient's religion - Catholic, Protestant, Jew, whatever. Once again the other aide explained the details. Some would have their arms by their sides; others would have their arms folded across their chests. By now I was getting more relaxed about touching the corpse, though I still got the willies if I looked at her face. I silently whispered a prayer that no one else would die any time soon.

Some of the pain I felt when seeing a patient die was left over resentment from my mother's death. Her life had seemed so unfair. I let my mind wonder to other things during the preparation of the patient so that I wouldn't have to think so much about the job I was doing. I remember that father had bought some land cheaply while my mother was still alive. He bought it for five dollars an acre. He and my brothers had cleared the land and built a house. They also dug a well. He started farming a portion of the land with potatoes and other vegetables. But we never did live at the farm. We were going to move in, but then my mother got sicker than she had ever been before. She never got to enjoy the new property.

A week after my mother had been buried, my father sent me to work in the woodmill in Lawrence. And so I worked and gave my pay to my father who would give me five dollars a week allowance. I always walked to work, but I still needed money for the bus to go roller-skating. Other than that, I had few expenses. Twice a year my father would take me shopping for clothes, just like when I was a small child. I didn't mind the way I was treated, since I didn't know any better. Then my father remarried. I really resented having a stepmother.

It was less than six months after my mother died. He gave his new wife everything. Even to this day I feel the same hurt I felt back then, believing my father had deprived my mother of so many things while showering her replacement with material luxuries. I resented living at home, but there was no way that I could possibly go out on my own. Never mind the fact that I had very little income. Decent girls did not live on their own in those days. They remained at home until they got married and set up house with their husbands.

I still managed to enjoy myself. I loved going to the movies with friends. We often went "dancing" at the roller-skating rink. Everyone knew how to waltz and jitterbug on skates! Funny how these kinds of random thoughts came into my head while I was working on the dead woman.

It was no wonder that I had some serious resentment inside me. Sometimes events at Danvers would bring all the old feelings back out into the open. At least some of the memories weren't all bad. Some weren't either good or bad – they were just thoughts from long ago. Like the memories of my mother's bird. My mother had had a pet bird at the time, a canary. I used to love hearing its friendly chirps. I'll never forget the day when we realized my mother had passed away. I spent the day in a daze of mourning and disbelief. When nightfall came I realized that the bird had not sung all day. Each day I would listen for his song, but he remained silent all through the wake. The wake was held in the home, with my mother's body on display in the living room. It was not until my mother's body had been removed from the house that I finally heard the familiar sound of her canary. I didn't feel sad or happy or anything in particular when I thought about that bird. In time, I came to have the same reaction to the deaths I saw at Danvers. That transformation chilled me, realizing how I was changing as time went on.

CHAPTER 6

Surviving the First Week

That first week was the hardest; I got physically sick. There was a lot of heavy manual labor involved in being an aide. Many of the patients required lifting to get them in or out of bed. I never realized how hard it was to dress a full-grown adult when that person wasn't about to help out at all. Sometimes my back would ache for an entire day. The fact that I wasn't eating well made matters worse, but I kept myself going.

I was only a young girl with a bad case of nerves that really upset my stomach. I had never experienced insanity or death up close or the multitude of ailments that can afflict people. The aides at Danvers were exposed to every human condition possible. I wasn't sure if I could really stay. But then the challenge of Steve's words would come back to me. So I stuck it out that first week.

At the time there were only doctors, RNs (Registered Nurses), and the aides. There were no LPNs, Licensed Practical Nurses, those with medical training but no formal degree. At Danvers there were only RNs who had college degrees and were allowed to do many medical procedures as well as handle staff administration. LPNs were nurses who were trained to perform a subset of an RN's medical duties. I learned that the aides called the managing nurses "blackbands". They were referred to as Blackbands because of the stripes on their nurses' caps that designated their position (the more stripes, the higher the authority). We would have to stand up when an RN or a doctor showed up. The relationships weren't casual like they are today. The girls used to say, "Blackbands coming." When the supervisors came, everyone stood up on the ward. When they left everything was quiet. It was almost a military deference to command. And the Blankbands almost looked the part in their austere, all-white uniforms. These women issued orders but otherwise kept their distance from the aides, fraternizing being an unspoken taboo.

Nurses' aides were given extensive training the first week. We were taught how to change beds, even if the patients were still in them. It wasn't so bad with the smaller, more fragile people. But some of them were heavy enough to strain even the male attendants. We needed to be trained in how to service the patients without injuring ourselves.

We were shown how to wash the patients with a quick sponging. Oftentimes there wasn't enough time to give every patient a full cleaning in the showers. We also had to learn how best to feed them, and change them if they had "accidents". We didn't have adult diapers. Sometimes they'd just move their bowels right on the floor (since some of them weren't wearing underwear). I hated when one of them would urinate in the bed, since then I'd have to strip the bed and the patient and clean the mess. I learned quickly where the cleaning supplies were kept.

After breakfast, most of the patients needed help getting dressed. Some patients didn't have full sets of clothes – just a sack dress. If a patient did have socks and panties, we'd put some on that came from a stash of clothing that we aides kept in a closet. The State did not provide individual clothing allowances for patients, and far too many of them had no relatives willing or able to provide them with anything. I was never really sure where these clothes came from, they were just items that showed up clean from the laundry room. Some patients had no relatives at all, at least any that came to visit, so we knew those people would need some extras.

We aides were also taught how to lift patients without hurting ourselves and how to watch guard over them when we brought them outside. We were given detailed instructions for individuals and their propensities for trying to escape or upsetting the routines. It seemed to me that the cautious guardedness of the staff was too extreme. It wasn't until later that I would learn to appreciate the strict rules for maintaining control.

Steve and I were living on Maple Street in Lawrence at the time. We both worked the day shift. We were trying to save money, so we tried for that week to see how it would work with us boarding at the hospital. Only adults were allowed to stay there, so Terry and Linda, our two young daughters, were sent to a home where children were cared for. The woman who ran the home loved children and took good care of my daughters. But it was still horrible. I wanted my children home with me. Missing them added to my miseries that first week. I was feeling stressed and guilty. The girls didn't seem to mind being away from me most of the time. I would see them as soon as I got out of work. Yet I was crushed by the idea of their being in someone else's home, and I could hardly wait for my mandatory day training to end. That's when I switched to the second shift. I would normally work from 6:00 p.m. to 2:30 a.m. Steve and I didn't get to see each other too much, but at least the family was together. And I was a much happier mother.

The duties on the second shift were different from that of the morning shift, but I quickly learned to adjust. Steve and I were so busy trying to keep our heads above water that we barely noticed how little time that we had together. Still, I managed to be happy in a carefree, "don't have time to think about things" sort of way.

CHAPTER 7

Getting Used to the "Normal" Routine

Although aides were assigned a specific shift, there was no set schedule for the week for which days to work or exactly what hours. Day shift meant you came in and worked between 6:00 a.m. and 6:00 p.m. filling in for other workers as needed. One day you might work 6:00 a.m. to 2:30 p.m., the next day you might get assigned to work 7:00 a.m. to 3:30 p.m., depending on what coverage was needed.

By this time I was working the graveyard shift, so my schedule was pretty consistent except when someone called in sick. It was easier to spend time with the children and my husband, although it took some time for me to adjust to going to work in the middle of the night and getting home early in the morning. The supervisor for each shift chose what days the staff had off, such as Monday and Tuesday, or Tuesday and Wednesday. Only the aides who had been there the longest got the weekends off. I used to get rides with other people until I got my own car. I appreciated the willingness of the other women to help me out with the transportation situation, but I had to work around their personal schedules. This meant that I often arrived early and had to wait around after my shift.

Early on I learned that we trainees hadn't been taught all of the rules. One time a group of us were in the kitchen. I didn't now at the time that we weren't supposed to touch the food in the kitchen that was designated for the patients. Everyone brought in his or her own meals. I didn't think anything of it when I saw the other girls occasionally eating food from the kitchen. One of the girls invited me to have something to eat. So, I made some toast, and just as I started to butter it, a Blackband came in unexpectedly.

She looked at me and said, "Hey Szot, what do you think you're doing?"

I said, "I'm having some toast."

That's when she asked me, "Don't you know that you're not supposed to eat the patients' food? So, what are you going to do?"

I looked at the bread in my hand that I was already buttering and said, "Well, I guess I'll eat my toast."

The Blackband gave me a nasty look, but then she just turned around and walked out. The other girls just stared at me. I had no idea that I could have gotten fired on the spot. And I certainly had no idea that aides never spoke up to the nurses.

There were strict dress codes back then, even for the aides. The nurses wore all white dresses. None of them wore pants. Even their sweaters had to be white. We did not have male nurses at the time, but the male attendants had to follow the same code as the women as far as the color of their shirts and pants. Even us lowly aides wore uniforms. We were required to dress all in white, too, even our shoes. Since I didn't own anything like that, I had to buy a few sets of uniforms with my first paycheck.

Each worker was assigned to a specific ward, but we worked every ward as coverage was needed (I worked only the female wards). There were male attendants to handle the men's and violent wards. Nurses avoided Danvers in those days, so there were very few and there was heavy turnover. This meant that the aides had to perform a large part of the work in caring for the patients. We were all pretty naïve, performing duties beyond the normal scope of our jobs just because they needed to get done and we didn't know any better.

How I longed to have my mother around to talk to at that time. Steve was wonderful and attentive, but I really wanted to hear her voice and learn her thoughts. Sometimes I felt overwhelmed knowing that my job had such an impact on other people's lives. Many of the patients could not perform even the most menial tasks. I felt responsible not only for providing the care essential to their survival, but also for adding some simple human pleasures to their days.

I had a rush of sad memories those first few weeks as I struggled to get used to this change in my life. My mind would wander back to the time when my mother was ill and needed my care, just like so many of the women I saw each day. I never regretted the sacrifices I had made for her.

I had dropped out of school in the eighth grade to care for my mother. This was not particularly unusual in my neighborhood since many children dropped out of school either to help at home or work at one of the local mills. My mother could no longer cook the meals and clean the house, so I took on those responsibilities. My father wanted me to go to work since I was no longer going to school, but my mother swore that as long as she lived I wouldn't have to go to the mills. And she kept her promise.

It broke my heart to see her slowly wasting away, grower weaker with time. I felt so utterly helpless. Perhaps that's one of the reasons I was drawn to nursing. Somewhere in the back of my mind I might have secretly believed that if I had known more about medicine I could have somehow stopped my mother's death. This was just one of the thoughts that would pass through my mind as I cared for other women who did not have daughters at their side to provide them comfort.

CHAPTER 8

Second Class Workers

The plainest fact about Danvers was that there was never enough help. There weren't enough nurses or even general help, sometimes. Things were hard because caring for the patients was so physically demanding. And with the shortage of nurses, aides were forced to take on more responsibilities. But, we were making good money; so we labored on.

Aides needed to learn some rudimentary nursing duties to support the overburdened professionals. The RNs taught us how to give insulin the old way using Bendix solution that had to be boiled in so many drops of water. We were taught how to measure the fluids and then to evaluate what we saw. We learned how to give out medication. The nurses would check the charts and place the pills in individual glasses for the aides to dispense at the appropriate times.

We were shown the violent wards to prepare us in case we were ever needed to work there. In the violent wards all the rooms were teeming with patients. These patients were like savages, really, like animals, when I think of it. We didn't have tranquilizers available to us, so we would just have to listen to their maniacal tirades. Nonsensical words would fill the hallways. Some of these people appeared so normal that it was disconcerting when they would start uttering sentences that had real words but made no sense, sort of like the gibberish of a two year old. Fortunately, I didn't have to learn why these were called the violent wards – that lesson would come much later. Still, even my short excursion into this nightmarish abode, devoid of coherency and reason, left me with an uneasy feeling. I had never before experienced the depths of madness. Over the decades I would come to learn all the disturbing places the mind can get lost in – places that harbored the darkest impulses, regions full of the bizarre.

Another tough lesson to learn was that even though aides were the lowest paid members of the staff, we were expected to carry the heaviest load. Sometimes some of the RNs would come in a bit tipsy. I guess they weren't thrilled about working at Danvers, either. We had one RN who had a real drinking problem; otherwise, she was very nice. She'd come in so loaded up with liquor; it would take us almost an entire shift to sober her up. The heavy smell of alcohol when she spoke would make me nauseous. We'd put her in a room and give her coffee and try everything to bring her out of it. We'd take turns walking her around the room in an attempt to get the alcohol through her system. None of us ever considered reporting her. We all just tried to make it through our shift. While she was out of it, the other aides and I would have to take care of the patients. Most of us were young girls (6 or 7 on the day shift, the number dropped for the later shifts); there were a few older women (past thirty). We younger ones took our cues from the older aides, following their lead. They all kept quiet because turning in a co-worker was something that was just not done – we had to stick together through whatever Danvers threw at us. It never dawned on me to complain to an administrator. So we'd have to provide all the patient care; that's one of the reasons why the senior staff decided to start teaching the aides the basics of nursing. No one spoke openly about the personal problems of the staff – we all just tried to function as best we could without causing problems for the patients. As long as the patients got the necessary care no one would rock the boat.

It wasn't just the professional nurses who looked down on the aides. During that time Danvers served as a training facility for some of the local nursing schools. The nursing students who came for training at Danvers looked down on the aides, too. We didn't like them because they treated us like dirt. They wouldn't even say hello to us or question us about any of our duties. The Danvers supervisors didn't want the students to associate with the aides. We weren't supposed to talk to the students. Naturally, I bristled against these artificial restrictions.

One day I asked one of the students if she'd like to see the very top floor, which was closed off. The workers had access to the attic, but there was seldom any reason to venture up there. There were beds with chains up there, relics from an even more brutal past. These were antique beds that hadn't been used in years, but the students didn't know this. That young student was eager to see the old attic, so she followed me up like an excited child. When we got up there she walked in first. The attic was stifling and dimly lit, eerily quiet compared to the constant noise of the occupied floors.

I slammed the door shut behind her and said, "Now try and get out!"

She had a passkey the whole time, as did all the staff, but she didn't know it would work on the attic door. I went back downstairs with her screaming for me to let her out. After a while, she figured it out. Surprisingly, she didn't turn me in. She was probably too embarrassed to admit an aide had gotten the better of her. I was able to play that trick a few times on the unsuspecting students.

Another time I asked one male student to help me out. He was young and had told me about his growing family. He was interested in seeing all the different parts of the facility, so I brought him down to the morgue. As we were walking down I told him that we always played a game down there.

"You open one of the doors where the bodies are kept and get on the tray and I'll shut the door. Then you knock on the door and I'll let you out. Then I'll get in!"

He was shocked. He honestly believed the aides had a warped sense of fun. We didn't really play in the morgue - but those students were so gullible.

Next, I mentioned to him that we stored meats down there in the big freezers. You'd think he would be suspicious by now. I knew he had a young family to feed, so I asked him if he'd like to take some meats home. I explained that we had excess that we stored down there and that the staff was allowed to take a certain amount home every month. He thought that was a great idea. Since we had our own kitchen and stored food for the patients' meals, he assumed that I was going to show him a normal freezer. Then I opened one of the freezers, which were used to store body parts, and asked him if he wanted an arm or a leg! He didn't know that when patients died, the doctors would often amputate hands or arms for later testing (if the patient had died from some disease) or training. Nothing like having first dibs on cadaver skin or skeletal parts! He still managed to laugh at the joke even though he was turning green.

My small but fun victories did give me some satisfaction. Yet in later years when I myself became a Blackband, I remembered the often demeaning treatment I had received as an aide. I learned that a little empathy goes a long way.

During this time I started making my own family traditions based on my work schedule. We would have our big family celebration on Christmas Eve instead of Christmas Day, since I would always be working that holiday. For Thanksgiving I would start preparing the turkey in the middle of the night when I got home, so that it would be ready for the table at noon. These are traditions that I keep to this day. Knowing I had such a wonderful home life made the working conditions a little less abhorrent. As the months passed I got to see just how bad they could get.

Patients weren't quarantined, so there were TB, syphilis, and every other imaginable disease congregated in the wards. Aides worked with every kind of disease. I was fortunate that I never caught anything or brought anything home! Still, I got an amazing training in medicine by being exposed to a wide range of human ailments. In those days we weren't required to wear gloves all the time when handling sick patients; I quickly got into the habit of washing my hands almost constantly.

Since we were so short on nurses, aides were taught how not only to give medication, but also how to give insulin. Rules today are very strict on who is qualified to perform certain medical functions and what the penalties are when those rules are broken. At Danvers, whoever was capable got the job. We were taught how to boil needles since we didn't have disposable ones. Of course, strictly speaking, aides were not supposed to offer any kind of medical services. It never occurred to anyone to notify the authorities. We appreciated the free education and the change of pace from our normal duties.

I enjoyed working with people very much, and I felt I had the ability to help sick people. I wanted to provide them with more than just basic life maintenance. So I decided that I could help people more and earn more money by becoming a licensed nurse. This was when Danvers started its own Licensed Practical Nurse (LPN) school. Here was an opportunity to learn a career, one I knew would mean more to me than just a paycheck. After discussing it with Steve, I enrolled in the program. This was quite an undertaking with a full time job, a husband, and small children.

CHAPTER 9

When Things Started To Get Interesting

With one hundred and fifty patients per ward, the staff was kept pretty busy, even on the night shifts. We aides would bathe the patients in the morning (usually just sponge baths) and dress them when clothing was available (otherwise PJ tops and johnnies which had been supplied by the state would suffice). Next we'd have to clean the porch and floors, wash the rooms, feed the patients their meals, and try to communicate and talk with them. After the evening meal, patients had to be changed for bed and given their final medications. Sometimes we'd braid the hair of the women. Add on the basic nursing duties we were learning, and that pretty much summed up the daily routine. At least on a calm day. In the beginning things ran smoothly for the first few weeks, making me forget that these people lived outside of my world.

The vast majority of patients were total loonies - once they were in they rarely ever got out. Yet there were cases of "dumping" - back then family members could have a relative committed against his or her will. These people oftentimes did not have a recognizable psychosis. Many times the doctors were too busy to review cases. And of course there were no doctors available on the weekends; for them it was a Monday through Friday job. That meant that admittance into the facility was rushed.

Although we had some fine doctors working the wards, Danvers had more than its fair share of men who just wanted their pay. I refer to all the doctors as "he" because at that time, all the doctors that came to Danvers were male. One doctor spent most of his time trying to make dates with the aides! His antics gave us a light topic to talk about during breaks.

When cases were reviewed, it was not so much to work out a treatment plan as it was to assess the patient's status. Mental hospitals were containment centers back then. There wasn't a goal of "curing" these people, at least not to the point where they could be functional in society.

I came to realize quickly how little I knew about human suffering. I'll never forget that bright, balmy day when I was feeling grateful to be out on the sunporch simply keeping an eye on the patients as they took in the warmth of the sun and freshness of the breeze. I noticed one patient seemed to be acting strangely, even for a Danvers resident. She was slightly twitching, and her face seemed to contort. She was an older woman, and I wondered if maybe it was a little too warm for her. Maybe she didn't know how to express herself. I had absolutely no clue, so I called one of the other girls.

"Hold on a minute, Szot."

I watched in mute fascination while I waited for the other aide. When she did come over, she casually stated, "Oh, she's having a stroke."

What's a stroke? I had never seen or even heard of such a thing. I think the other aide was amused by my complete lack of exposure to the many hazards of life. She calmly explained what a stroke was as she rang the emergency bell so the patient could be rushed out for medical treatment. I learned later that the poor woman ended up paralyzed on one side.

Treatment for mental illness was limited. Medication consisted of aspirin and blood pressure pills. Shock treatment was actually performed, but patients would have to be dragged in, and the aides would practically have to sit on them. The doctor would put a stick in the patient's mouth to keep her from swallowing her tongue. Then he would place electrodes on the temples and start the juice. The first time I saw this procedure I was horrified. There's a certain smell that lingers in the air and seems to stay with you long after the patient has been returned to her bed. The fear in the eyes of the patient seems to jump right out at you. Creepy thoughts would enter my head. Could I ever find myself strapped to one of those tables, watching as a stranger sent searing jolts of energy into my body, making me lose part of my memory, part of myself?

There were also the "Cold Sheet" and Tub treatments. The former consisted of wrapping a patient very tightly in cold sheets. These were sheets that had been placed in refrigerators until they were needed. I got goosebumps each time I had to wrap a patient up in one like some kind of modern day mummy. This supposedly reduced agitation and cleared the brain.

The latter treatment, innocuously called the Tub treatment, consisted of having the patient sit under continuously running water - even during meals. The patient would spend an entire day sitting naked in a tub. This treatment was used to help calm a patient down. Neither one of these treatments helped my nerves as I watched in silent fascination.

I was seeing so many things that I had never imagined. Each time I thought I had seen the worst, I was thrown into something even more bizarre. But instead of wallowing in self-doubt, I became stronger, learning to accept the tragedies I faced. I was becoming a part of Danvers. The ancient walls were becoming familiar. The smells and sounds of the place were becoming normal to my senses. Still, Danvers guarded many secrets, some painful, some joyful. The longer I stayed, the more she revealed to me.

I learned the depths of my own empathy and pity when a man was brought in who had the face of a twenty-one year old, but under his clothes he had the body of a ten year old. He had to have a catheter (a tube inserted in his penis) for his urine. The young man's father worked for a school. This diligent father scoured all the sources he could find to learn of any advances that could somehow improve his son's existence. He managed to get his son attached to a machine that could be used to operate other devices through facial contortions. That patient needed to be hand fed like a small baby. After meeting that man I raced home to hug my own children, grateful that it wasn't one of them in that situation.

I somehow managed to survive my first tumultuous year and actually started enjoying working with the patients. The aides quickly developed a tight camaraderie. It was not until I became pregnant again that I considered giving up this type of work. That turned out to be a short-lived doubt about what I was able to handle.

CHAPTER 10

The Expanding Family

I had never considered it odd that I was a working mother. My sister-in-laws all stayed home with their children. That was typical for most wives following World War II, at least the ones from middle-class families. Having only one of us work had never been an option for Steve and me. I had worked outside the home right from the start. Of course, Steve and I were an unusual couple for that time for many reasons.

I met my husband during World War II when he was in the Army. Even though his sister, Ann, was married to my brother Larry, I had never met Steve. One day, Ann brought Steve over to meet me when he got back from service in Europe.

At the time, I was dating a jockey from Rockingham Park in Salem, NH. Steve showed up in uniform. He was a really nice looking guy. We met in February, then wrote to each other until he was discharged from the service in June. We were engaged in July and married in October. Everyone was convinced that I must have been pregnant to have such a short courtship.

Our marriage caused quite an uproar in the family for another reason, too. At that time, Italian girls married the Italian boys their fathers chose for them. Steve was Polish. Up until then, I had obeyed my father in everything. He would not forgive this affront to his authority. Marrying a Polish boy meant I had to pay my own way for the wedding - my father refused to even acknowledge the pending marriage. I paid a total of five hundred dollars for my wedding dress and reception. Unfortunately for us, there was a bus strike going on, so not all the guests we invited could attend. We ended up with four hundred and eighty five dollars in wedding gifts. And so we started our life together, full of confidence and fifteen dollars in the hole.

It seemed like we spent the first years of our marriage always on the edge of that hole. I remember when I was in the hospital for my third child, Paul. Health insurance wasn't common and HMOs didn't even exist. Steve gave the admitting nurse one hundred dollars and told her to send his wife home when that was spent. That pretty much wiped out what little money we had to spare. I needed to return to work.

That's when I started to seriously consider a career in nursing. I could make far more money as a nurse than as an aide. Heck, I was doing most of the work anyway. Luckily, Danvers State was opening the door for anyone willing to make the effort with its new nursing program.

CHAPTER 11

Becoming A Nurse

Before I even considered working at Danvers State, I had been interested in nursing. I even learned some of the basics of medicine. One day I had seen an advertisement in the paper for the Wayne Correspondence School. It offered training in nursing using courses through the mail. It said a high school diploma wasn't needed to become a licensed nurse. I applied and began studying through them. Although the assignments I submitted all received passing grades, I felt as if I didn't really understand what was being taught. I could memorize answers, but I didn't really understand the "why" of what was being taught. After a while I dropped out. But, I never completely gave up on the dream. I worked as an aide for ten years, never forgetting my former aspirations. Then Danvers reawakened the dream.

There was a severe shortage of nurses, RNs. There weren't many of them. Back then, the pay for educated nurses was pretty abysmal. The staff needed help, so the aides were allowed to apply for the new Licensed Practical Nurse training program. I figured, why not get extra pay? If I'm going to do the work, I might as well go to school for it and earn the extra pay, which I did. The schooling was held right in Danvers State, but we were taught by a special teaching nurse hired from outside.

Before we were allowed to start training we had to take an aptitude test, regardless of past experience. Then we needed to get the results signed by several doctors, and have pictures taken. We had to train on our own time; I worked on the day shift on the evenings that classes were held. Steve worked nights so that someone would always be with the kids. Even if daycare were available back then, we definitely would not have been able to afford it.

Even though we had to go to school on our own time, it didn't cost us anything. It was only part time, just a couple nights a week. Since Steve and I had only one vehicle, we decided that he would drive to work and I would carpool with some of the other aides. That was a big mistake. My shift started at seven in the morning, so I had to be ready for my ride by quarter past six. After working a full day and going to school for several hours, some of the girls wanted to go out drinking! I got dragged along a couple of times, sipping cokes and waiting impatiently to get home. I couldn't take it for long, so I started taking the car. Most of these women were single. I had a husband and children to worry about. I wasn't interested in hearing the latest gossip about which doctor was sleeping with which nurse. I also wasn't interested in bar hopping. It wasn't so bad once I started driving myself into work. Steve didn't mind if he had to stop for a drink after work with the guys he carpooled with!

So we aides went to school for almost two years, and when we were through, before we graduated, we had to go to the statehouse. If one were 39 and under one had to take an oral and a written exam. If one were over 39 years, only a written test had to be taken. I had to take both.

One week a group of aides went and took the written test. We went in from nine in the morning until noon, then had one hour for lunch. Then we went back in from one until three. Three weeks later we were sent a notification of what our grades were, and then we had to go back to the statehouse where we were taken for our oral examination if we had passed the first part of testing.

There were four doctors there who asked us questions. Each doctor was assigned to so many candidates. We were divided up by the first letter of our last names. There were candidates from all over the state. After that, we just waited. If you passed you got your certificate. I passed! I earned my nurse's license. Then they started paying us as LPNs.

There was a graduation ceremony held at Danvers. I wasn't able to attend. I had sick children that needed my attention. Still, my husband was full of pride. I only wished I could have shared the moment with my mother. Each of us was given a nurse's pin and two stripes to put on our nurses' hats. One was blue and one was gold, the colors of Danvers State. Right away I went out and bought some uniforms. Nurses uniforms were traditionally white dresses back then. Slacks and colored clothes weren't allowed. I bought several dresses, several pairs of white nylons, some white cardigans, and a pair of white nursing shoes (these had special sneaker-like soles).

I was so proud the first time that I went to work in full uniform. Imagine me, the daughter of immigrants with little formal education, having a real profession. My father and brothers had never encouraged my dreams. But they were still proud of me. Of course, Steve was happiest about the increase in pay. Seems like we were always struggling with money matters.

That's how I finally made my dream come true. I had tried the Wayne Correspondence School, but I didn't care for it because I didn't understand a lot of it. I needed to see things for real and have hands on training.

When I went to school in Danvers I had already experienced a lot of the things being taught, so it was a cinch for me. I saw a baby being born. A patient stuck his hand through the window - the whole palm of his hand was sliced open. The specialist invited me into the operating room to observe. He told me that the torn hand would eventually look just as good as the other hand - and it did. A patient stuck a piece of a safety pin inside her vein, and I saw the doctor operate on that. I saw a patient stick scissors in her side. We saw a lot of things, things that were really unbelievable. So when I went to nursing school it was nothing for me. We were fortunate to be allowed not only to observe everything, but also to assist the doctors. As aides we had been taught how to give insulin, how to take blood pressure readings, how to take temperatures, to give injections, and to give out "meds". Since I was already familiar with all of that (from my correspondence school studies and working as an aide), it was very easy even before the nursing classes.

Now the real challenges would begin. The new nurses were expected to take on more responsibility than they had held as aides. We were also expected to be available as needed. This meant working several different shifts in one week. That would wreak havoc with my sleep. Still, I was just so happy to be a real nurse that

I didn't mind the inconveniences. As an LPN, I was higher than an aide was, but the RNs were still the supervisors and managers. Of course, that didn't mean that an LPN didn't get stuck being the sole authority for an entire ward for an entire shift on occasion!

Changing from an aide to a nurse didn't change everything for me. I had reservations about modern medicine's capabilities. And I didn't always take everything the doctors said as the gospel truth. That's because I knew that sometimes the science and medicine didn't always have the right answer. I learned that from a childhood experience.

I was in second grade when I contracted rheumatism. One morning my mother woke me up, and I told her that I couldn't move my legs. She asked me what I was talking about. Then she rolled me out of bed, figuring I didn't want to go to school that day. When I hit the floor and couldn't get up, that's when she realized I had a problem. She put me back in bed and called the doctor. He could offer little help. So I remained bedridden. I was terrified by the thought of never walking again.

Then my eyesight disappeared. This frightened me even more than losing the use of my legs. I had to drop out of school. My parents had called in several physicians by this time. None could provide any possible treatments. My mother spoon-fed me during that time. After six months my eyesight came back. Just like that.

Although my blindness was temporary, I still could not walk. The doctors gave my mother no assurances that I would ever be able to walk again. They all said there was nothing to be done. Finally, this one old lady, a friend of my mother, came to the house.

She said, "Teresa, go to the drug store and buy mustard plasters. Buy small ones. They're only about fifteen cents apiece."

My mother bought two and put one on each of my knees. This was in June. The old lady told my mother to put a blanket on my knees. She said that in two weeks, when the mustard plasters fell off, I should be able to walk. And that's exactly what happened. For two years prior I had not been able to walk.

It took quite some time for me to recuperate from my illness. Although I regained full use of my legs, my eyes had been permanently damaged. I would find this out much, much later in life when I had difficulty seeing.

Eventually I was able to go out and run around with the other kids in the neighborhood. My brothers used to let me play football with them. My mother would chase them off with a broom when she thought their roughhousing was getting too aggressive for me. She always tried to protect and pamper me.

After that experience, I made sure to listen to the old women and their home cures.

A Now Deserted Ward
Copyright Jeremy Barnard 2004

Kirkbride Building
Copyright Jeremy Barnard 2004

A Patient's View
Copyright Jeremy Barnard 2004

The A Wing
Copyright Jeremy Barnard 2004

CHAPTER 12

The Reality Of Being A Nurse

One thing that didn't change when I became a nurse was the forlorn atmosphere of Danvers. It was in the late 1950's that I started working as a nurse. The views of and care for mental illness were dramatically different from what they are today. We spent most of our time providing medical treatment and basic care. There was very little attention given to treating mental illness. Dementia was still something society refused to face. So those who couldn't function "normally" were condemned to the dim corridors of Danvers. Hope was never really part of the treatment.

The facility was divided into front wards and back wards. I worked the female sections. B1, B2, and B3 were admitting wards. C1, C2, C3, D1, D2, and D3 were front wards, also known as parole wards because the patients were allowed to go out onto the grounds during certain hours of the day. A1, a back ward, was used for the extremely sick, those patients who needed constant care. A1 annex, another back ward, held the old and feeble as well as those suffering from severe dementia. A3 was a securely guarded ward used for violent patients. The back wards, such as A2, were also called the closed wards, meaning the patients were allowed out only in the bullpen, a fenced yard with someone always in attendance. Visitors could come and go in the front wards during visiting hours much like visitation at a regular hospital. The rules were different on the back wards; visitors had to be let in and let out by the attendants. In the back wards, if a patient behaved well, he or she was allowed to eat in the cafeteria if an attendant went along. The remaining patients would be fed on the ward.

Looking back at my time at Danvers, some of the things we did seem archaic. Even after all the medical advances of World War II, we still boiled syringes and reused them. They were thrown away only if they broke (which sometimes happened since they were made of glass). Tongs would be used to pull them from the boiling water to prevent contamination. Nothing was disposable back then. And there was hell to pay when something did have to be thrown away. There was always a shortage of money for running this huge facility. But at least we had most of the modern conveniences, like refrigeration.

Refrigeration had been something unfamiliar to me when I was growing up. The iceman would bring melting blocks of ice to the apartment. We kids used to like watching him haul the huge block on his back, trying to get it to us as quickly as possible. This would go in the icebox to help keep our perishables. Though, with six brothers, food usually didn't sit around very long! So, with all things being relative, I thought Danvers was state-of-the-art when I worked there!

Often times we would have to treat chronic illnesses such as diabetes. Our methods of treatment were actually considered advanced at the time. Bendix was boiled over a Bunsen burner. A few drops of a patient's urine were added to test the blood sugar level. The color would change; we would determine the units of insulin to inject based on the color. This had to be done before every meal for all patients known to be diabetic. There was one patient who was so diabetic that the solution turned bright orange (which was extremely bad). It turned out she was cheating on her diet. She would pilfer food from other patients. Keeping close watch on her during mealtimes became another duty. Yet, she still managed to sneak in some contraband on occasion.

We also had to deal with patient self-abuse. To get attention, sometimes a patient would mutilate him or herself. Despite our vigilance, a patient would on occasion get hold of something that would prove quite destructive. One time a patient broke off the end of a safety pin that had fallen to the floor unnoticed. She stuck the sharp end into her arm. Fortunately it didn't hit a vein. A doctor was called in; he searched the arm to locate the metal, sealed off the area, and cut the needle out. We always had to be in a state of watchfulness.

Sometimes Danvers seemed more like a penitentiary for violent criminals than a health facility. The patients often had fights with each other. Not just arguments or loud altercations. They would lunge at each other in death matches. They would need to be separated. The women would tear at each other's hair and scratch at each other's eyes. And there were the nurses and aides, acting as referees, sometimes getting battered just as badly as the patients were.

So much of our time and energy went toward controlling the patients. Before the introduction of tranquilizers, patients were locked in rooms when their behavior got too much for the staff to handle. Control through medication did not start coming into use at Danvers until the 1950's. New drugs were tried out on patients. Sometimes a patient would have the opposite reaction to a drug than what was expected. A tranquilizer could actually make a patient hyperactive. One female patient was able to smack open a security door after being injected! It took ten male aides to get her controlled.

Controlling the patients was actually one of the more pleasant aspects of working in the old facility. I discovered that fact one day while checking on one woman who was in seclusion, a heavily used practice before the introduction of behavior modifying medication; some of the patients were like animals, and this was the only method of control that provided reasonable protection for the staff and other patients. I went inside the room. The patient stayed way in the corner while an aide and I tried to clean out the room. There were urine and feces on the floor. When I looked up, I saw these things flying.

I said, "What the heck are they?"

The other girl with me said, "Cockroaches."

"That big? They look like little birds practically."

I got so scared I said, "I'm not going in that room!" Fortunately, the aide didn't mind the huge insects, so she finished the job.

Angelina Szot and Barbara Stilwell

There were cockroaches on the porch as well. These were huge ugly black things that seemed to have no fear of people. The porch was a long windowed area that afforded the patients some fresh air and sunshine. The porches were locked areas with bars over the windows. Sometimes the patients weren't taken to the bathroom when they needed to go once they had been taken out to the porch because some of them didn't have the presence of mind to ask to be taken to the lavatory. When the need arose, they would just defecate in the corner. Then the aides would have to clean the whole porch. In the summer time, the aides would turn all the benches over and use a bucket of bleach and a fire hose to clean them. They would open the sewerage vents. There would be hundreds of roaches scattering about once the benches were turned over. The aides would throw the straight bleach on them and then wash them into the vents with the hose. That was how everyday porch duty went for whoever got that unlucky assignment.

There were still between one hundred and forty to one hundred and fifty patients per ward, male and female. The staff kept mighty busy feeding, washing, dressing, and medicating them. There were 12 female and 12 male wards. J3 was the violent ward for men and A3 was the violent ward for women.

With so many people crowded in, it was not surprising when small epidemics broke out. There would be dozens of diarrhea cases at one time. The patients would be brought several at a time into the showers and literally hosed down to clean the filth. It didn't hurt them physically in any way. Some of them were dying from dehydration caused by the diarrhea. All the clothes were soiled at one point, so most of the patients had nothing to wear. I remember telling my husband there wasn't a patient on the floor who had a stitch of clothes on. Danvers had its own laundry room complete with staff for washing bedsheets and patients' clothes. Sometimes a diarrhea epidemic would create such a pile of rancid, filthy clothes and sheets that it would take the crew several days of bleaching and disinfecting to get back to normal.

In between the normal activities (if any of it could be called normal), the staff would have to deal with inspections. I'm talking about years ago, when oversight of such facilities was fairly lax compared with today's standards. Whenever the bigshots from the state health department were coming, there would be all new dresses, new everything for the patients, the best of meals. Then the next day, we would go back to the old routine. We used to take the extra beds we had dragged out for the inspection and put them back in the attic. There had to be so many beds required by law, and beds had to be so many inches apart. We used to have to open and close wards to hide the patients because Danvers was so overcrowded. There was never enough money to improve the situation, so we just did the best we could to pass the inspections and try to give the patients decent care.

By this time my family had grown to three children. We spent some time living in the Beacon Projects in Lawrence. This was a Government housing project that charged rent based on income. It was a lovely place to live, with plenty of young, struggling families who maintained their homes. There were community activities such as dances, and the neighbors really went out of their way to be friendly.

We also started enjoying the benefits of two incomes. I never had a television in the house while I lived with my parents. It was a luxury item even after I got married to my husband. Some of the neighbors eventually got sets, and it was a real privilege to be invited over to see one of those magical shows. We eventually got ourselves a color set. Life just couldn't get much better.

CHAPTER 13

Starting A New Decade

Years ago, when people were put in Danvers, they were usually forgotten. Sure, there were the lucky few whose families diligently paid visits and brought them things. Sadly, that was the exception; a majority of the residents were abandoned. No visitors came to see them; no relatives or friends monitored their treatment or progress. It used to be that family members could easily have someone committed for a "rest". That meant the person lost a huge part of their lives. The hospital used to take a new patient's license, savings books, false teeth, glasses, and jewelry. These were put into protected storage. Some of the patients from the old countries who couldn't speak English didn't want to take their rings off. They knew that once their precious belongings were out of sight, they might never be seen again. The patient lost all rights, even the right to vote. It was still this way at the beginning of the 1960's.

There were treatments in use at the time that now seem outrageously horrible by today's standards. One of the worst was shock treatment. Shock was horrible. Patients were dragged in. Somehow they all knew what was coming. I felt so sorry for these poor, terrified people, but we were taught that this was a necessary part of their care. We were forced to harden our hearts in the belief that what we were doing was for the best. Electrodes were placed on the body, and then electricity would be applied. The patient would shake violently. Tongue depressors were put in their mouths to keep them from biting off their tongues. Patients would actually break bones from their wild thrashing during shock treatment. Sometimes there would be six nurses holding a patient down. It was mostly used for really depressed patients. It was believed that it changed the brain pattern. It would make them forget whatever it was that was making them depressed. None of them ever forgot their session with the electrodes. Often it was the family that would initiate this kind of treatment. Next of kin could request specific treatments be administered. If a patient had no family, he or she would be almost a guinea pig for various treatments, including shock. The doctors would evaluate the patient's behavior after treatment to see if it had any effect. I often had a difficult time accepting what I saw. It was as if the staff had frankensteinish good intentions – they honestly thought they were helping the patients and humanity as a whole. The ends justified the gruesome means.

Drugs were starting to come into common use as a way to control and treat the patients at this time. Control through medication did not begin coming into use at Danvers until the 1950's, and became a regular part of care in the 1960's. Pentathol and Thorazine were used often. Thorazine was used to sedate patients so they wouldn't realize they were going through trauma. Pentathol was used to get reticent patients to talk. Drugs became standard tools in our daily care.

My duties at Danvers remained pretty consistent over the years, even with the dramatic changes in the use of medications. Where once we would isolate and restrain patients who were severely disturbed and posed a threat to themselves and others, we now administered drugs that altered their behavior, and sometimes their personalities. And, as always, the doctors would conscientiously record all patient reactions to medications. Only the mute walls of the asylum stood witness to the bleak misfortunes of these tortured people. Still, drug therapy was a vast improvement over older forms of control.

Before the introduction of tranquilizers, patients would be locked in rooms when they became too much for the staff to handle. A terrified patient would often become even more disturbed and frenzied in the confinement of the locked room, with his or her screams of fear and frustration echoing through the corridors. At least that horrifying aspect of care was slowly phased out as drug use became more prevalent. New drugs were tried out on patients, usually without their knowledge, and never with their consent. We weren't required to get it. There were no watchdog agencies vigilantly ensuring patients' rights. Our guiding principle was to do the best we could with whatever means were available. Still, during this time we gained invaluable insight into the many new "wonder" medicines.

When the medication treatment didn't work, there was a help call bell system used for those emergency situations when extra help was needed. Help call was used originally for fires. A certain bell would ring on each floor telling staff members where to respond. Most of the time it was the violent ward; once in a while it was the admitting floor. When the call came through, no matter where you were or what you were doing, you had to stop and go because it meant someone was in trouble.

During this time male and female patients were kept strictly separated. When the patients were brought downstairs to eat, the nurses and aides had to patrol the tunnels because the women weren't allowed to talk to the men. Of course, our limited staff could not keep an eye on every single patient every minute of the day, so the patients always managed to pull some stunts.

Sometimes a guy patient would say, "I'll give you a cigarette. Want to give me something?" to a girl patient.

The girl would say, "All right, you want a feel or something?"

Then when she'd stop, he'd give her a cigarette. We'd usually let these small transgressions slide when we did catch them. We knew there was no way we could stop people from interacting, and living in Danvers seemed punishment enough. So we just tried to keep them apart as best we could.

Someone would always have to walk the patients through the underground tunnels to go to the cafeteria. There were bars dividing the men and women. They weren't allowed to openly talk to one another - but they could see each other. They'd be on their own sides. There was mesh on the dividers. If the patients were well enough (even some of the violent ones) we'd let them go to "Caf". Someone else had to bring them back to the wards and check them in following meals. They had to be checked in and out to make sure everyone was accounted for. It wasn't one on one - so many patients were assigned to each nurse or aide. So you had to really watch yourself because you never knew when they might turn on you. Knock on wood I never got hit.

Sometimes you'd have a patient from a back ward that was a little off center, nothing too severe, but sometimes they'd go off their rocker and start acting wildly and you wouldn't have the help to back you up. On the violent ward there was this one stocky girl I'll never forget. Everyone was afraid of her. She grabbed the food truck one day (the truck was used to bring food to the patients who couldn't go to the Caf - it was sent out to every ward - the girls would have to serve individual meals to those patients). The girl picked up the whole cart with everything on it and flung it across the room. That's how much strength some patients could have.

We had to take care of patients' personal hygiene, since most were incapable of really caring for themselves. Once a week, patients would be brought down for a shower. Two girls would put on bathing suits and bring the patients down. We'd wash then all down. As soon as we got through we'd say, "Next." They'd leave - then there would be girls on the other side who would cut their fingernails and toenails, brush their hair and give them clean clothes; whatever we had for clothes! Those patients who were too sickly to be brought down to the showers were given sponge baths in their rooms.

The hustle and bustle of caring for the patients was not our only concern. As a state facility, we had to worry about operating expenses. Every July first came the start of the fiscal year. By that time Danvers would have used most of the funds allocated by the state. Come the end of June we'd go around collecting everything, trying to save this and save that. We'd save anything because we wouldn't get any new supplies until about maybe the middle of July. This meant hoarding tongue depressors, gauze bandages, whatever. And if you wanted a vacation, you never took it the first of July because lots of times you didn't know if you were going to get paid or not. We didn't know what the state's budget would look like. You had to hang on to your vacation.

As the years started to go by, things slowly began to change, progressing a little at a time. Where at one time we had mainly medical doctors who would tend to patients' physical needs, we now had professionals in psychology and psychiatry reviewing cases. One thing that didn't change was the shortage of people willing to work at Danvers. After getting my license, my duties changed - but sometimes we were so short of help that everyone had to pitch in to do everything. It wasn't a matter of what you wanted - it was a matter of what you had to do. One time it would be just me and another girl and the patients on a ward. We had to feed them by ourselves (we were on a ward that required a lot of personal care). The patients were really good - if we treated the patients kindly (the more stable ones) they'd help us out with some of the necessities - they'd do anything for a cigarette, a cup of coffee, a piece of candy - just little things meant a lot to them. I always brought cigarettes in.

I used to buy a carton a week even though I didn't smoke! It didn't seem strange at the time since smoking was an accepted practice at Danvers just as it was allowed at regular hospitals. I'd also bring in candy. The patients would show their gratitude for these little displays of kindness by helping us. And so somehow we managed to keep everything running.

CHAPTER 14

And Life Goes On

My last two children were born in the early 1960's. I had one of the most terrifying experiences at Danvers at this time. Betty was a young patient. She always made me feel a little nervous. She never said much, but she would constantly watch every little thing I did. I had also heard stories about her, about how she didn't know right from wrong and had a temper that could flare up at any time. One day I had to bring her to the medical building for a dentist appointment. We used one of the underground tunnels connecting the buildings so we wouldn't have to go outside.

She wanted to visit someone in the medical building, but I said, "No you can't. You have to go to the dentist. Those are my orders."

She responded, "All right."

Her curt reply didn't sound convincing. I had a queasy feeling that things were not all right. It seemed like a never-ending walk through the dark corridor, but finally we got on the elevator to go down. I was pregnant with my fourth child, about three months along. Everyone at Danvers, including the patients, knew this. We came down the elevator, each in our own corner of the tiny confines. I was terrified, but I couldn't let it show. That was a cardinal rule for all the caretakers.

"You know Mrs. Szot, when we get to the bottom they could find you dead, you and your baby dead."

"Betty, when the elevator gets downstairs they'll find three dead bodies. I'd never want to fight you, but if it comes to my life I'll beat the shit right out of you."

We got to the bottom and got out of the elevator, and Betty casually asked, "I guess I can't have a smoke now?"

"Of course you can." I gave her a cigarette.

"Will you buy me a Coke?"

"Yeah, I'll give you the money for a Coke." How could a person jump from bizarre threats to the mundane almost in the same breath?

She went to the dentist and when she came out she said, "I have to go right back."

"That's right."

Her calm composure only added to my anxiety. Naturally when you're scared and walking those featureless tunnels it seems like a thousand miles. We got back on the elevator in the same corners.

Betty repeated the same threat. "You know Mrs. Szot, you could end up at the top dead, you and your baby."

"Do you think I'd just stand still while you beat me?"

We reached the top and got off the elevator. "Well I guess you're going to tell and have me put in seclusion."

Almost all patient transgressions resulted in seclusion. "No, why should I tell, it's only between you and me."

She figured I would still tell. But when another nurse asked how she behaved, I said just fine. Betty never forgot. She was always good to me after that. Years later, I ran into a liberated Betty at a downtown Lawrence store. I had my youngest daughter with me. She looked Betty up and down.

"Hi Mrs. Szot, how are you?"

"Ma, who's that lady?"

"Oh, an old friend of mine."

With the birth of my last two children, there were now five children in the family. By this time my oldest two were teenagers, so they were able to help with the care of their youngest three siblings. Things hadn't changed much as far as my working conditions in the fifteen years since I had started working at Danvers. I sometimes had to pull double shifts when staffing shortages got really bad. Once we had a storm that lasted three days and three nights. The weather was so bad that many of the workers couldn't get into work. Those of us who were already there had to work around the clock. We took patients out of their rooms to help. We told them that they needed to help; for us to survive everyone had to pitch in because we were so short on staff. They pitched right in, washing dishes and cleaning rooms.

One of the things that always weighed heavily on my mind was the fear of bringing something contagious home to my family. Staphylococcus, tuberculosis, and syphilis were prevalent. At the time we didn't know how to treat all of those things (the medical world did not know how to take care of everything). So, we didn't segregate sick patients according to their diseases; all contagious patients were quarantined together. There would be various illnesses on a ward. We were supposed to wash our hands and wear a gown when working with staph cases, but rules weren't enforced. I always made sure I washed constantly (even if a patient weren't contagious), and I made use of the masks and gowns for whatever protection they might give me. As years went by things started getting better and better. We learned new methods for controlling outbreaks, and we were given new medicines for curing these often gruesome illnesses. Through it all, I managed to keep from contracting anything or bringing it home to my children.

As my family had grown, I had become more and more aware of how other families treated their kin. The patients often didn't come with suitcases of their own clothes. They came with just whatever they happened to be wearing when they were brought in - their families didn't usually supply much. If a patient had relatives, he or she might have an occasional visitor, but those that didn't were forgotten. Lots of people would just bring a sick relative up there and erase them from their lives. It was very easy to get in, but it was hard to get out - not like today.

If a husband said, "My wife's crazy", then there was a good chance he could have her committed. He had to get a doctor to sign (attest) to it. It was a fairly simple matter to force an evaluation. Once a person got up there the staff examined her, and if they thought she was sane, they'd say to her husband, "I'm sorry but your wife is sane. We're not going to keep her." And then they'd let the person out. But if there was any doubt about a person's stability, that's when they had to worry. Years ago it was very hard to get out once someone was committed. There was a mixture of mental illnesses suffered by the residents; some were really just cases of depression, but these would be thrown in the mix with violent, completely insane individuals with no hope for a cure. As years went by the staff started doing better in evaluations and treatment. But, in the early 1960's, mental illness was still a frightening business best left out of the public consciousness.

There was one attractive young woman who appeared to all the world completely sane. She was polite, courteous, and educated.

One day I asked her, "What the hell are you doing here?"

That's when she told me about her husband and children. She had had a beautiful family.

She told me, "When the war came, my husband told me that he was going into the service, so I threw my kids out the window."

No remorse, no regrets, just stating the facts. How that small exchange made me want to rush home and hug my own children.

Another horrific crime was committed by a woman named Mary. She told me how she ended up at Danvers. She used to babysit for her sister. One day she got sick of it all. She wanted to get even with her sister, thinking she had been burdened long enough with her sister's child. So she put the small baby in the oven. When her sister got home she told her that she had made supper. Hearing tragic stories like this made me appreciate the safe haven I had waiting for me when I got home.

Even with working full time, I always managed to make homemade meals for my family, sort of my way of showing my love for them. I had learned how to make my husband's favorite Polish dishes, and I taught myself how to make Italian sauce and American Chop Suey. Still, my husband sometimes had to make the meals. He would create strange concoctions from whatever was leftover in the refrigerator.

Sometimes a person would come to Danvers who was a terrifying reminder of how insanity can lie just below the surface. A pretty young woman named Diane was one such person. Her life was pleasant and for the most part uneventful until she brought another life into the world. Then something dark and frightening, something that must have always been there, came into the light. Do we all have something cowering in some blackened corner of our minds, something that needs only the right key to unleash it?

Diane was one of those rare true psychopaths. During the second review and evaluation, Diane was classified a paranoid schizophrenic. She was committed. She spent many years as a resident. Sometimes she'd be angry and scream justifications for her actions. At other times she was remorseful and contemplated suicide as a fitting punishment for her horrific acts. Always these dramatic moods would fade with time, and Diane would go on with her daily business of living.

Diane was a twenty eight year old woman who had married a man twenty four years her senior. She was talkative and friendly, and homicidally insane. She felt no compunction about telling us the details of her heinous crime. Shortly after her marriage she became pregnant. Following the usual course, she gave birth to a beautiful baby boy. Seven weeks after the birth she committed the unspeakable. She believed the world a maudlin place full of misery. She felt the child had nothing in life worth living for, so she had to release it from its misery. She stabbed him seventeen times with a pair of scissors. The first person to discover the tragedy was her mother. Diane was immediately sent to Danvers State and admitted, before any authorities were notified. The baby had not yet been declared legally dead because no doctor had verified death. Once Diane was on state grounds, the police couldn't touch her. There was no need for an arrest or a trial to prove insanity if she were committed.

At the time, the state recognized only two types of mental patients - schizophrenic and suicidal. Whichever staff member admitted a patient had ten days to interview and evaluate his or her condition then present an opinion at Staff Review. The doctors saw a patient at most twice before the Staff Review. Legally, Diane couldn't be committed because she didn't fall into the established categories. Yet clearly she was a demented individual. Even the other patients avoided and shunned her. The decision was made to release her.

As soon as Diane left the hospital grounds, a police cruiser was waiting for her at the bottom of the hill by the entrance. The police picked her up and whisked her to jail. When her case was brought before a judge, the court decided that she needed a thirty day evaluation, so she came back to Danvers. This time she was committed.

Once a resident at Danvers, she would never have to face judgment for her act. Eventually she was released. The state could never take her to court again because she had been found insane at the time of her crime.

This was a real learning experience for me. I had been sheltered from some of life's harsher realities. And since my mother had died so young, I was left in the dark about a lot of things. One of them was marital life. I brought a deck of cards along on my honeymoon with Steve so we would have something to do! Steve was understanding about my naivete. His years overseas during the war had given him some insights about life (and women). We went to Boston for our honeymoon. We stayed at a hotel for three days. During the day we went rollerskating and out to dinner. I thought I was experiencing life to its fullest. Still, Steve had never prepared me for the dark tragedies I would witness at Danvers. No one could have prepared me.

CHAPTER 15

The Routine Life of a Nurse

After so many years working at Danvers, I thought for sure I had seen everything. Yet, there were always surprises that I would never have imagined in a million years. Even the hourly patient checks could be amazing. I went to check on one recently committed patient who was quiet and pretty much a loner. She was singing Rock-a-bye Baby. Her singing was very pleasant, though it seemed odd. The other nurse and I looked in and saw her rocking what looked like a doll. When we approached to see how she was doing, we saw that she held a real child. She had delivered her own baby. The evidence of the birth was smeared on her bedcover and dressing gown. No one had known she was pregnant. It took a few moments for me to really understand what had happened. Of course, the child had to be taken away from her. That really broke my heart because I could see that she loved her child. But I also knew she was incapable of caring for it. I never found out what finally happened to that baby. It was just another heart wrenching incident that added to the underlying sadness that in many ways defined the facility.

It was as if the bright sunshine of day never thoroughly entered Danvers. Even with all the progress made over the years, there was still a pall that hung over the sprawling structure. Some of the inhabitants seemed to have a gloom that followed them around from their first day there. Mary was violent from the day she had arrived at Danvers. She was brought to A3. She often tried to escape. One time she almost succeeded. We eventually located her still on the grounds. After we brought her in, a full body search was done on her, which was mandatory in such situations. She was stripped and searched, then thrown into a locked, padded cell.

Immediately she started shouting, "You bastards! I'll fix you, I'll fix you!"

Well, she had a match stuck way up her vagina. She must have somehow pulled it out in tact and dried it off. Then she lit the room on fire. She lit a mattress and started hopping around yelling, "Whoo, whoo!" The fire department was called in. We pulled her from the smoke filled room, gagging from the acrid stench.

Most of the time we managed to do a pretty good job during routine searches.

One time, a husband and wife were admitted. During the standard search, over one thousand dollars was found tied around the husband's waist in a money belt. The wife had claimed they were broke. I guess they were looking for free room and board for a month. Indigents were allowed to stay at Danvers during an evaluation with their expenses paid by the state.

Even after all those years, the method of feeding the patients at Danvers remained the same. Food service provided family style bowls of food in the cafeteria. The nurses and aides had to make the patients trays individually. I always found it odd that that never changed.

Steve, my husband, was still working at Danvers, too. He went to the violent ward. I warned him that those patients could throw anything. Naturally, my big, sturdy husband thought I was exaggerating despite his many experiences. That was until he met Mary. One day on the ward, Mary had thrown the hot food wagon, just picked it up and flung it. Then she picked up Steve and flung him. The other guys were too afraid to go in and help him. Fortunately, one of them hit the button for the emergency bell, and soon most of the staff was on the violent ward. Steve learned his lesson that day. He never underestimated any of the women after that.

Most of the wards held non-violent patients, and even the patients on the violent wards tended to be well behaved. So, dangerous incidents (at least for us) were rare. Sometimes it was the patients who didn't fare so well. The nurses and aides were often overworked and in a rush. They couldn't always give the patients the time and care they needed.

Of course, the majority of nurses and aides were truly concerned caregivers; they would just get tired sometimes. Then there were the few who should never have been allowed into the profession. There was one senior nurse in particular whose cruelty to the patients still causes a rise in me to this day. It was almost as if she would take pleasure from tormenting those people who needed her most. There was one old woman who she would intentionally get all riled up. Once this woman had been worked up to the point of screaming, that nurse would call the front office to complain and demand medication. After seeing this go on, I decided to quit because it made me sick. I didn't dare reprimand a senior nurse. It just wasn't done.

The head administrator called me in to her office and asked why I was leaving. I said I just wanted to leave. She pressed the point, and I said I hated seeing the patients mistreated. I told her everything. It was as if all my frustrations were released in a torrent of anger. The administrator patiently listened to my tirade. I half expected to get fired for my display. Instead, I was told that my concern was truly appreciated. The adminstrator made sure that someone else was assigned to that particular patient after that. It seems outrageous today that such acts of maliciousness would go unpunished, but back then the ever pressing shortage of help forced the administration to deal with the staff in the best way possible short of firing someone. I later took that nurse aside and told her that she would get hers someday and end up alone. And that's just what happened many years later.

Staffing did eventually improve, especially after some improvements to the facility itself. The operating room for medical emergencies had at one time been on the ward at Danvers before the facility was remodeled; after it was remodeled, we had a beautiful place called the Medical Building with several Operating Rooms and really good doctors started to come in. We could not handle all medical situations. Girls who were pregnant would be shipped off so many weeks before their due date to Worcester State because they had the facilities needed to handle pregnancies. Then, so many weeks after the patient gave birth, she'd come back - but without the baby which would be put up for adoption. The authorities didn't assume that the mothers would eventually be released and would want their children - they weren't sure. Years later, the policy was changed and mothers were allowed to choose, raising the child through the state until the mother's release. The baby was a ward of the state until it was decided that the mother was ready to care for herself and her child. Sometimes this took many years.

Back in those days, smoking was a common, accepted practice. I didn't smoke, so I got to watch guard for the Blackbands while the other girls went into the kitchen and smoked and drank coffee, a quick ten minute break. One day I didn't bother giving them the alarm. I was tired of always getting stuck alone on watch. They all got caught and reprimanded. I raced downstairs and hid down there for a while because I knew there would be hell to pay. Later I nonchalantly told them that I hadn't noticed the supervisor coming.

And so the time passed, and I came to accept as normal all the bizarre behavior of the patients as well as the quirky habits of my co-workers. I enjoyed my job and somehow managed to keep the rest of the family happy. My two oldest daughters had by now graduated from high school. Both of them applied for jobs at Danvers. Terry got a job as a nurse's aide, and Linda got a job as a secretary in the administrative office building. My middle son was already in high school.

CHAPTER 16

Progress In And Out

As the years went by, medical knowledge improved and so did the lot of the patients at Danvers. Laws governing admittance and release made it much more difficult for families to dump unwanted members. Still, there was always a perpetual shortage of funds and the continued dread of mental illness meant a shortage of staff. It was as if Danvers were locked away in some slow motion time warp while the rest of the world raced on.

At home I was enjoying the benefits of having two paychecks as well as two children working. My husband was always one to try the latest things, so we got to enjoy a large color television. It was quite a sensation in our home. I remember I owned my first television after I married Steve. Back in the early days the T.V.'s were black and white with small round viewing screens. Early on I learned my husband loved any new gadget or gizmo – which turned out to be a life long interest. So naturally, we had to have "color" – this meant placing a special material over the screen to give it some color. Part of this sheet was red and part was blue producing a strange hue on different parts of the screen, but at least it wasn't just black and white. Since there was no cable, we relied on a "rabbit ear" antenna that constantly needed adjusting. It had been a truly great luxury for us!

Televisions were available in Danvers on the sunporch. These were on shelves high up on the wall. And they were inside cages to keep them from being broken whenever a patient decided to start throwing things. There were still occasions when patients would go berserk. No amount of medication or monitoring could suppress the violent outbursts. Sometimes it seemed like we were not making any progress in dealing with insanity. Danvers watched silently as we struggled each day to master the human condition.

CHAPTER 17

The Whole Family Sees the Inside

After my two oldest daughters graduated from high school in the early sixties, they both got jobs at Danvers. It was wonderful having my daughters working with me. But, that meant that I now had to work out a schedule to ensure that my two youngest had someone to look after them. I also needed someone to care for our dog – I adored that animal and refused to give it up. He was a white German Shepherd that I had gotten from a friend who trained those dogs for local police departments. I wanted my children to enjoy having a pet. One of my fondest memories is of the "pets" my brother Freddie kept when we were children. Although we never got a puppy or kittens, Freddie did manage to capture and tame quite a collection of animals. There were pigeons, ducks, and chickens. His favorite was a squirrel. One day the squirrel scampered onto mother's shoulder and down her dress. She rammed a broomstick down her back to get it out, howling at my brother the whole time.

That poor squirrel flew out and ran off. Freddie somehow enticed his little friend to come back eventually.

I was determined to make everything run smoothly despite the fact that four of us would be working full time. So, I worked the night shift with my oldest daughter, and my husband worked the day shift with my other daughter who worked in the office. Linda didn't see too much of the happenings at Danvers working in the Administration Building. Terry got to see it all, working as an aide.

One day, Mary, the patient who had shocked my husband Steve with her strength and dexterity, had to get an EEG, a procedure used for checking the heart. We didn't have the equipment for this, so we scheduled an appointment at a local hospital. Before sending her to the hospital, the doctor had given Mary 1000 mg of Thorazine and a shot of God only knows what. He then gave my daughter Terry a prescription to be given to the nurse at the hospital who was authorized to give Mary more Thorazine if she acted up.

At the hospital, Mary was brought into a small room with racks of records lining one wall. An elderly woman technician came in and began to put probes on her head. Mary reached up and pulled off all the probes. Terry asked the technician to get some male nurses, one with a syringe. She knew that Mary was the kind of patient who would hit you until she figured you were dead, literally.

"Mary, if you get one step off that chair, see these racks, you're going to wear them!" Terry screamed.

The law at the time prevented any type of assault against a patient except in self-defense when it was a matter of your life or theirs. Terry figured that that was one of those qualifying times. Fortunately, she was wrong. Still, I could see how much the incident had shaken her when she returned to tell me the news.

Terry got another fright out in the yard that was used in the summer time. A fourteen-foot fence topped with barbed wire surrounded the recreation area known simply as "the yard". The patients could sit outside and smoke, or just enjoy the sunshine. Once a patient started a ruckus by screaming at the top of her lungs. This was a woman who used to pull out her own fingernails. Even the seasoned nursing veterans were nervous around this patient. One of the novice aides got petrified when she heard the almost inhuman screeching. Terry held one arm of the patient and told the novice to hold the patient's other arm while she got her keys out. She wanted to bring the thrashing, screaming woman inside. The patient let out a piercing scream that shocked the novice. The girl panicked and let go of the patient's hand. Quick as lightning, the patient grabbed at the base of Terry's hair. Terry realized she was going to blackout because the pain was so bad, so she punched the patient with all her might, and they both went down together. Just then one of the nurses came to the door with some male attendants. As Terry got up, the patient tore her side buttoned uniform. It took some time for my daughter to stop shaking.

There was another patient I'll call "T" who showed us that we could sometimes expect the unexpected. "T" couldn't be trusted. She was a drug addict, but she was not violent, just mischievous. One night Terry and I were stuck working the violent ward doing a double shift. I was cleaning the medicine cups, which were glass back then, in the medicine room. I was preparing to "do meds". Terry was just opening up the first door in seclusion, her duty for the night. She needed to do a check of all the patients. She asked "T" if she were going to behave. "Yeah" was the noncommittal response. Terry asked her if she wanted a smoke. "Yeah." So Terry handed her a cigarette and invited her to go along on the round as she opened all the rooms except Regina's. Regina was in total seclusion all the time. So Terry let "T" out. She worked her way down the hall. I was at the other end. "T" at that moment was standing behind a chair. I was coming out of the kitchen with two racks of glasses. Just then I slipped. I was going face first into the glasses. Terry never had a chance of reaching me in time. Suddenly, "T" shoved the chair in front of me. I smashed into the chair full force, but the glasses shattered harmlessly on the floor. It gave me a huge bruise on my side, but otherwise I didn't get a scratch. It proved my theory that if patients were treated like people, they would respond to you with their own version of humanity. Most times a cigarette and a cup of coffee were all that they wanted. Sometimes Terry and I got reported to the RNs for overindulging the patients (i.e., giving them too many butts even though no one was concerned about cancer back then). Some of the administrators believed that the patients would become unruly if some of the staff members gave them things and others didn't.

Fortunately, my daughter and I didn't get assigned to the violent ward very often. My husband Steve, on the hand, being a heavyset man towering over me at six feet, got violent duty quite a bit. Since the pay was good for the time, none of us ever complained about the hours or the duty assignments. But even the "regular" wards had their share of exciting moments.

Once, while Terry was playing cards with a couple of other girls during her meal break, we got quite a shock. The staff had just gotten paid. I was playing cards, too, and I was winning. Just as I collected another winning hand, a supervisor came in and asked if we had checked the patients in their beds. I asked Terry if she had checked the patients. She said she had, but the supervisor said that a patient had just called from Lynn stating she had taken a cab to the city to visit friends. She needed money for the cab fare to get back! I didn't get into trouble for the incident, but I gave Terry and the other aides hell because it was their responsibility to ensure the patients were in their beds. The state ended up paying for her cab fare!

The next day we needed help with breakfast (there were almost eighty patients that needed to be individually fed; some only needed a food tray delivered, but others needed to be spoon-fed). There was just me and Terry and a young aide to feed the patients. Only one room was locked. That patient always had to remain behind a locked door; all the other patients were free to roam the ward. That patient locked up was thin and wiry, but she was violent, grabbing your hair if she got the chance. We asked some of the patients to help. They distributed food and washed dishes. We gave them change for the vending machine and cigarettes (the two cartons a week I would bring to work barely covered such occasions). The next shift was amazed at how organized the ward was once they realized how short-handed we had been.

By this time, my family was living in a house in Groveland, Massachusetts. It seemed like a mansion to me. Growing up in my father's home was quite different. My first memories are of when we lived in an apartment in nearby Methuen. It was extremely small and cramped. Back then we didn't have the money for many of the things that people find common today. During the summer months we ran around without shoes. Shoes were too expensive for play. There were no such things as sneakers. Just before school started we would each receive one pair of shoes for school and church. Now my children were living in a real home and enjoying things I never even dreamed about. We had an above ground pool in the back yard. After working the night shift, Terry would often invite some of the other young staff members over for a late night swim. Steve installed floodlights for these impromptu parties.

With four working adults in the family, we were able to live comfortably. My youngest two thought I was making up stories when I would tell them about what life was like when I was a little girl. When I would take my youngest daughter shopping for clothes I would tell her what it was like for me. My father took me and my brothers shopping for clothing only twice a year. My father would pick out the dresses I would wear for the next six months. We would go to the stores in downtown Lawrence, walking the entire length of Essex Street to find the best bargains. I had to be very careful not to get rips or stains, since there would be no replacements.

Linda enjoyed working in what was considered a modern office environment. The hospital wanted to make a good first impression, so the administration building was always kept in top shape. Linda rarely ventured onto the wards.

Linda was the first to find work elsewhere. Eventually Steve learned electronic plating and took a job at a company that made computer boards. Terry, who always loved to cook, found a job at a restaurant. I would eventually move on, too.

CHAPTER 18

Holiday Spirit

Some of my happiest memories of my time at Danvers are about preparing the wards for the holidays. My favorite holiday was Christmas. It didn't matter to anyone what their religion happened to be – we all enjoyed the light-hearted spirit of the season. There were no organized Christmas activities for the staff, so the nurses would put on their own Christmas party at work. This was a small celebration, but we enjoyed it immensely.

The hospital did sponsor a holiday event for the patients. Only the front wards had parties, not the back wards, like A2. These were small affairs – a small tree and some gifts for the patients. The hospital would pay for this from a holiday fund. Different people from Raytheon and Western Electric would bring in presents for the patients – soaps and booties and things like that. The Telephone Company donated the best gifts. There would be warm gloves, mittens, and stockings. The women would receive slippers and fancy manicure sets. Supposedly the back ward patients were considered too excitable and uncontrollable, so they were never given any sort of celebrations. They would just be given their allotted gifts with little fanfare.

I worked on a bad ward in the back, A2. Nobody wanted to work on it because sometimes the patients needed to be tied down, they ate bizarre things (like their own blankets), and were very messy. There was one patient who would eat anything near her mouth, including her blanket. When she defecated, there would be a chain of a ball, a string, a ball, a string - really fascinating! The hospital administration didn't think these patients understood about the holidays or even cared. The staff knew better. We could see the anticipation and excitement on their faces. It was like the reaction of a very small child who doesn't understand everything but can still enjoy the wonderful sights and sounds.

When the staff on A2 decided to have our own celebration, we pretty much had free rein to do as we pleased as long as our work got done and we didn't create any fire hazards. We washed the walls, really scrubbed them down. We even made curtains for the windows. We needed to because the ward was so drab. The floors and the walls were a dull white – everything was antiseptic. Everyone pitched in, RNs, aides, even some of the kitchen help.

People who came onto my floor, whether they were visitors or staff members, were shocked by how wonderful and festive the ward looked.

We wanted to include the patients in on the celebration. We let all the patients out of their rooms so they could see how nicely their home was fixed. Then we decorated for Christmas, hanging strings of paper rings and putting up decorations that we had bought with our own money. After that, we dressed all the patients in their best clothes. We worked our buns off, but it was worth it. A2 was just a back ward, ignored by most. We were determined that the residents would not be forgotten on this holiday. Finally, I pulled out an old phonograph that I had brought from home; we played every Christmas album I had brought in. Of course, Bing Crosby and the Andrew Sisters were my favorites, so everyone had to listen to that album a few times.

Every Christmas there was an open house for families and the bosses. When people came to A2 they couldn't get over how clean it smelled. All the patients were up (some in adult high chairs). We had even hung decorations from the ceiling. I kept that record player going during the entire visit.

This became an annual event for A2. The patients often wanted to help with the decorating. We tried to let them participate to the best of their abilities. The joyous mood seemed to do more for their health than all the medications they were given. I know it certainly made the holiday season a grand time for me.

Sometimes I would bring my two youngest children, Barbara and Steve, to Danvers for the holidays. My children loved going up to the asylum! They knew the people were "sick", but they didn't understand that they were insane, most likely never to live anywhere else. The aides would make hot cocoa for my children. The patients would play games and do puzzles with them. The kitchen staff would make dishes of cookies and special sandwiches for lunch. Some of the patients would even make homemade presents. One elderly woman knitted a clown doll for my daughter. It was a genuine work of art. The woman had worked tirelessly bringing the colorful yarns together. For years it was displayed on my daughter's bed, a cheerful reminder of her visit.

The children loved the Christmas holiday the best. I took Christmas Eve off to spend with my family at home, because I always worked Christmas Day. When the children came on Christmas Day, I would play children's Christmas albums on the record player that I had brought in. I believe the patients enjoyed the time with the children the most, singing Christmas carols along with them and watching the excitement on their young faces when they got any presents.

The staff also celebrated Thanksgiving at Danvers. A really special meal was served up by the kitchen staff – everything from soup to nuts. The hospital paid for this special treat. The staff would put up decorations for Thanksgiving and Easter. The patients all seemed to appreciate the extra effort we made for them.

CHAPTER 19

The Staff

The staff was constantly changing at Danvers, but some, like me, were long-termers. There was a time when some of the best surgeons in the area worked at Danvers. This was after the new medical facility had been built for Danvers. This pristine addition contained the latest equipment. Danvers policy allowed for the use of the most avant-garde techniques to be used. The staff there would handle most of the routine medical care and some operations. After the new medical building was running, we would bring in outside doctors for certain special operations that were beyond the capabilities of the regular surgeons. Before that, if a patient needed an operation that the regular staff could not handle, the patient would be sent to Hunt Memorial Hospital in the city of Danvers. Now Danvers State could compete with other facilities as far as what she had to offer doctors. Her reputation changed after the renovation – she was no longer a place to be avoided.

As the years went by, the doctors who were the best in their fields stop coming to Danvers. The staff was still well qualified, but Danvers couldn't offer the money or prestige that the new doctors wanted. They could easily find the same top quality environment at more main stream facilities. There were still lots of internships. These were not just general practitioners. We were lucky enough to get a variety of specialists. They would stay so many months, then venture on. Some would accept permanent positions at Danvers.

When I first started at Danvers in 1948, we had some of the worst doctors around. No "serious" physician wanted to work at an insane asylum. They would work only Monday through Friday. Often times we would get doctors who couldn't get jobs at other facilities. This quickly changed for the better. Still, for the longest time all the doctors were male, and all the nurses were female. That did not change for a very long time. Danvers was a reflection of the society it served.

There were doctors, nurses, and aides of all ages. There were a lot of smokers. Smoking was restricted to certain areas. Everyone was allowed to take smoke breaks, so I would have to stay on the floor and keep watch since I never smoked. It seemed perfectly natural to see the doctors discussing patients over a couple of butts and cups of coffee!

A few of the nurses and aides were working at Danvers just for the money. They didn't really have a great concern for the patients' wellbeing. They were downright mean to the patients. But, if they got caught – heaven help them! They wouldn't get fired unless they posed a threat to a patient. Instead, they would get assigned the worst shifts and the vilest tasks, and get stuck pulling duty on the holidays. A severe tongue lashing often went along with that!

I would get a real laugh watching some of the doctors making passes at the pretty young nurses and aides while they made their rounds. It was a regular "Peyton Place" at times. Everyone knew my husband, Steve, so I didn't have to worry about any unwanted advances.

Some of the staff had worse problems than the patients. Over the years there were aides who had problems with drugs. And nurses who had problems with alcohol. We never snitched on each other. We always tried to cover for anyone who showed up at work unfit for duty. That was an unspoken rule we all lived by. If a nurse showed up with a few too many under her belt, one of us would start a pot of coffee and keep feeding it to her while keeping a watch over her until it was safe for her to go on the ward. We always made sure staff members were fit to tend their wards.

Many of the aides held more than one job in order to make ends meet. They often lost a lot of sleep. When exhaustion finally caught up with them, we would let them sleep it off. All of us understood how hard it could be to manage. Still, we made sure that anyone who wasn't capable, for whatever reason, did not deal with the patients. It made for more work for the rest of us, but we just considered it part of our responsibilities.

The staff members socialized quite a bit outside Danvers. We would sometimes stop for cocktails after our shifts or meet for dinner at each other's houses. My children received Christmas presents from some of my coworkers. This camaraderie made Danvers an even bigger part of our homelife. Strange how the brooding presence of Danvers so easily got incorporated into our lives, forming a unique bond between the people who spent a large part of their lives inside her walls.

CHAPTER 20

The Routine Continues

In between the holiday festivities, life would go on as normally as possible at Danvers. One time on A3 a patient had taken a pot and began beating (more like clobbering) most of the day staff. The second shift refused to go in. That was the night Terry and I got stuck working a double alone. Sixteen hour days were rare, but they really took a toll on me. I would be completely exhausted. Thank heavens Terry and Linda were old enough to help with the housework, childcare, and cooking. Even my husband, Steve, would pitch in with the family meals. He would concoct strange entrees from whatever leftovers he could find in the fridge. Sometimes they would come out amazingly well. Other times we had to force ourselves to eat whatever he invented. It really didn't matter after a hard day at Danvers.

Even as medical knowledge and equipment progressed, we still had to face the reality of death from time to time. Even in the 1960's, nurses and aides were responsible for prepping the bodies for the morgue. Whenever a female patient passed away during one of my shifts, I would be reminded of my own mother's passing. Which isn't surprising considering the old traditions that made a deep impression on me that would keep the memories vivid for my whole life. The wake was held at home, as was the custom back then. For three days and three nights my mother's body lay in the parlor while friends, neighbors, and relatives streamed through with condolences and dishes of food. All the Italian families in Lawrence knew one another. During the wake, some of my brothers' friends who used to hang out at Petralia's market showed up with a tree that they wanted to dedicate to my mother. It was so large, they couldn't get it up the stairs to the apartment. They ended up leaving it at the bottom of the stairs, in the hall. It had a card on it that said "From the boys on the corner". Sometimes I'd go out into the hall to look at the tree and get away from the sight of my mother's body. Those three days seemed like an eternity.

There were regular hospitals at this time with television in the individual rooms, but Danvers wasn't that lucky. There were very few luxuries for patients at our kind of institution. Not only did our residents have to deal with ravages of the mind, they often had physical complications that added to their miseries. What we did have were patients with fungus - any kind of disease - you never knew what you could get. We had to handle people with puss filled lesions on their bodies. Knock on wood, I never got anything, even though I dealt with just about every communicable disease around.

Even after my many years at Danvers, I remained wary of the violence that could erupt at anytime. That was one thing that never changed about the place. There is the memory of the time a patient attacked my daughter Terry in the Bullpen. After yanking at her hair so hard that Terry suffered headaches for several weeks, the patient was restrained by several male attendants and remained subdued after that. This was not unusual behavior for some of the more violent patients. Even so, Terry and I always treated the patients as human beings. We understood that they could not always control themselves. They could do the most vicious things without intentional malice.

We continued to use help calls when situations go out of hand. Everybody available would come running when one of these calls was made, usually from A-3, the female violent ward, or J-3, the male violent ward. One time a patient got hold of the food truck, lifted it over her head, and was threatening to throw it. Male help call was made because this woman could not be handled by the female staff. We did out best to keep her from hurting other patients or us while we waited what seemed like forever for the men to show up.

Danvers was still being used as a training facility for nursing and medical schools. Years ago, nurses had to go to school for three years. The last three months they had to spend at Danvers. If they didn't successfully complete their training at Danvers, they had to stay another three months. Then they would be assigned to hospitals after training. Even in the late 1960's, the nurses who worked at Danvers were considered lower quality than hospital or private care nurses because they worked at a mental institution. The students were only allowed onto certain wards during their training. This practice continued right through the 1960's. Even though I had gotten my nurse's license, I had to put up with the condescending attitude of some of these young students.

One of the students I really liked was a young man named Bill. He was always pleasant and courteous, eager to learn whatever the experienced nurses had to teach him. Bill was one of the ones I used to tease about the "game" of taking turns pushing each other into the body drawers down in the morgue. I'm not really sure if Bill knew I was just joking. Anyways, I would patiently show the students how to insert IVs and catheters. I'd teach them how to dole out meds and take blood pressure. None of them considered working at Danvers. They all wanted to move onto "real" hospitals. So I would let them practice using ace bandages and tongue depressors, all the while knowing that most did not consider their current patients anything more than things to practice on.

Occasionally I would work the day shift, but for the most part I continued working nights. Paul, my middle child, was well into high school, and Linda had gotten her first apartment. Although things were changing rapidly in my home life, work at Danvers remained consistently the same.

CHAPTER 21

Kids on the Ward

With my unconventional work schedule, I sometimes had my two youngest children come to work with me after school. They didn't mind it at all; they thought of it as an adventure. They actually preferred coming to the "nut house" rather than staying with their sisters, who were even stricter than I was. Danvers State was a collection of old brick buildings that looked almost like a mansion or a castle. The kids loved exploring the grounds and peeking into the dark, hidden places that were part of this impressive structure. When my husband got off duty, he would bring the children home. This was during the late 1960's.

The patients enjoyed these visits as much as the children did. Many of them had no contact with people from outside the hospital. No family or friends would visit. Some of the patients were simply old and tired, a little forgetful, but not insane. Spending time with my children would brighten their days. The children would play board games or make puzzles with the patients. Some of them would ask me when the children would be coming. These little visits were big events. But, the children were never allowed onto the violent wards. They were only allowed to interact with the more sedate residents.

Sometimes my youngest daughter, Barbara, would go off with her father to the ward he was working on. Both my husband and daughter loved playing word games and working on huge jigsaw puzzles. They didn't mind playing with the patients. When Steve had some chore to do, he always kept an eye on Barbara.

Even the other staff members seemed to like having the kids around. At least no one ever complained. Often the young aides, who were really only children themselves in their late teens and early twenties, would tell the children jokes or buy them candy bars. I would sometimes get out my huge ring of keys and take them to some secret place (like the attic).

I always made sure that the children were kept far from harm's way. Some of the patients had contagious diseases. Others were so far removed from reality that I was afraid the children would be disturbed if they tried to start up a conversation. So, I limited their contact to those patients I knew were safe. I always kept checking on the children when they did leave my sight.

Holidays at Danvers were much more fun when my children came to visit. They so loved to help with the decorating. It gave Barbara a special thrill to help pass out the cookies the kitchen staff baked. The kids would play records and dance around. At Christmas time they would receive many small presents, oftentimes hand made, from the patients.

The grounds of Danvers were especially appealing to small children. There were ancient oaks soaring skyward with their broad expanse of leaves. The grass lawns were well maintained. There were paved walkways between the stone buildings. Looking up from the front courtyard, one could see the myriad of windows staring back from the face of Danvers. Sometimes patients would gaze out these bar-covered windows to watch my children performing cartwheels and running races on the freshly cut lawn. Some watched with joy, reliving the exuberance of their own youth. Others seemed to mourn the passing of their carefree days.

These visits from the children were always brief, just the time from the start of my shift until the end of my husband's shift. This was usually about two hours. Having this overlapping work schedule and being able to bring my children to work saved us the expense of babysitters. Also, there weren't daycare centers easily available like there are today. Even if these had been available, I

Angelina Szot and Barbara Stilwell

think I still would have preferred having my children experience the interaction with the people I had come to know so intimately.

CHAPTER 22

Leaving Danvers

By 1970 I was sick of everything. The pay raises were awful. Back then nursing didn't offer the good wages available today. This was before the nursing strikes of the 1980's that forced hospitals and institutions to reassess the payscale for nurses. And because Danvers was a state institution, there wasn't enough money to improve compensation. I thought I could do much better at a nursing home.

Also, the care provided by the staff was sickening me. It seemed as if the new employees hated their jobs and the patients under their care. Some of the aides would ignore patients who had wet themselves. They'd leave them for the next shift to worry about. Even the nurses seemed to lose sight of the fact that these were people. They treated them like just a job to be done. That's not to say that there still weren't some fine and caring people out there, they just didn't seem to apply to Danvers.

Finally, I thought the working conditions would be better somewhere else. Pulling double shifts was taking a real toll on me. And keeping an eye on the aides was a job in itself.

It was a tough decision to make. Danvers State had been a part of my life for over two decades. I had a lot of good memories and good friends there. But, I knew I needed to make a major change in my life. And I knew I didn't want the hectic pace of a city hospital.

I decided to apply to nursing homes since I was very familiar with geriatric care. There had been many patients at Danvers who suffered from extreme old age, nothing more. So, I applied to a nursing home in Lawrence and got accepted right away. With some sadness I turned in my resignation at Danvers in 1972.

CHAPTER 23

Patients After Danvers

Several years after I left Danvers, I read in the paper that the had state decided to release some patients from Danvers State into halfway houses. It was touted as a real step forward in the management of mental illness. Other patients were placed into nursing homes. The facility was eventually closed. This was the start of a dramatic change in the approach to treating psychological problems. It also signaled a societal shift in the way people viewed sicknesses of the mind.

It's been three decades since I left Danvers. Many of the people I knew back then have passed away. Yet the memories of that time are still vibrant. It was odd to see a mention of Danvers in a recent edition of the Eagle Tribune. The paper had a quote from State Senator Frederick E. Berry. He was lamenting the fact that many of the stone markers identifying the graves of patients buried at Danvers had vanished. "We showed no value for these souls. We dumped them in fields, covered them up and walked away." Now these people are the unknown dead. His comment is equally applicable to the people who had lived there. They were the unknown, forgotten living.

ABOUT THE AUTHOR

Angelina Szot is a retired nurse living with her youngest daughter in Hampstead, NH. She had always dreamed of publishing her collection of stories from her time at Danvers State Hospital. She finally made it happen in time For her 78th birthday.

Barbara is a Principal Systems Engineer with BAE Systems in Merrimack, NH. She grew up hearing stories about Danvers State Hospital and even spent time at the facility when her parents were working there. She has two children and three step children who all live in the area. The two youngest, Tommy and Angie, love to hear Grandma's stories about working at an asylum. To them, these stories seem like bigger fantasies than anything at the cinema. Barbara believes her time spent at Danvers State Hospital has helped her immensely in her current job.

Eileen is a neighbor friend of over ten years who is an educatorin the Haverhill Public Schools in Massachusetts. Barbara's and Eileen's children, Jonathan and Christina, also share a friendship. Of course, thesefriendships grew over the years from shared family events where Barbara's mother, Angelina, was always at the center of Danvers State Hospital storytelling. Eileen recalls public school field trips to Danvers State.

Made in the USA
Lexington, KY
12 July 2010